To Tom,
Bright Blessings
all - ways !
Love
Cynthia

Butterfly Moments

A COMPOSER'S JOURNEY TO SPIRITUAL ENLIGHTENMENT

by Cynthia Jordan

Cynthia Jordan
2137 Office Park Dr. Suite A
San Angelo TX 76904
www.cynthiamusic.com
325-942-6757

© 2003 Cynthia Jordan
All rights reserved
IBSN 1-59196-940-9

Cover and Book Design by Wendy Byle
Wendy Byle Design
Woodland Hills, CA

Editing by Sarah Fisher

*Butterfly Moments is
lovingly dedicated to my
beautiful daughter Denise Michelle.*

Table of Contents

Introduction 4
Me, Myself and I 8

Cindy Jordan

A Musical Childhood 16
Through A Child's Eyes 23
Be Kind to Your Waitress 28
Jose Cuervo 34
Jose Cuervo lyrics 40
After the Surrender 41
Forgiveness 47

Miss Cindy

Cowboys, Cuervo and Texas . . . 54
The Voice 60
The Day I Learned
How to Pray 65
The Bookstore 70
The Airplane Ride 75
From the Other Side 79

Cynthia

Peaceful Journey 86
The Magic Music Well 95
A Journey In Time 99
Journey of the Dolphin 105
The Quiet Journey 112
The Celtic Journey 119
New Beginnings 126
A Time of Peace 131
Butterfly Moments 137
Elusive Butterfly 144

Butterfly Moments of Inspiration

United We Stand 146
Invisible 151
Healing with Music 156
The Rosebush 160
Sacred Sex 164
You Make Beautiful Love
With Your Eyes 169
In God We Trust 170
A Final Note 174

Introduction

*"A musician must make music, an artist must paint,
a poet must write if he is to be ultimately
at peace with himself.
What a man can be he must be."*
—Abraham Harold Maslow
(Motivation and Personality 1954)

As I tried to stand up in the Critical Care Unit waiting room, at Sumner Regional Hospital, I felt my knees buckle and my legs go out from under me. I was weak with worried anticipation and as I began to collapse, my friends Derri and Karen caught me by my arms. After a horrific ordeal that seemed like a living nightmare, my daughter, Denise, was in very critical condition in the next room.

Some people think about ending their life. Some people actually do something about it. When we found her, it had already been eight hours since she "very calmly" ate over 500 pills in the darkness of her room. We would later learn that in the last few months, Denise had been involved in a series of dark events that she had kept secret to herself. Her existence had spiraled down to what she saw as her final option. That night, when she went to bed, Denise was determined she would never wake up again.

The last time I had gone in to see her, with the exception of her chest barely moving up and down, all signs of life were virtually gone. Her blood pressure was crawling at 48 over 18 while at the same time her heart was racing at 150 beats a minute. There was a huge tube down her throat, breathing for her through a machine. You could hear the ventilator keeping perfect time with an eerie kind of swishing sound, in the corner of the room.

My poor, sweet baby! Denise was only seventeen years old and so beautiful. Her long blonde hair cascaded over her pillow and her fair skin was cold to the touch. There were several tubes protruding from all parts of her body, monitoring her vital signs and feeding medicine into her veins. She looked very peaceful and free of pain, but it was obvious to me she was not among the living. I could feel she was at the threshold of death's door and there was nothing I could do. Or was there?

Denise had given us a scare once before when she was five. A young horse had kicked her in the head and knocked her out cold. That was the day I learned how to pray. Now at 3:30 p.m., January 16, 2003, as the snow fell quietly on the ground, I was praying again for the life of my little girl. "OK", I told myself. "You've been talking the talk, now it's time to walk the walk. Surrender and trust! This is too big for you! Remember your oneness with the unconditional, loving God. Where there is Love, there is no pain and *God is Love*. It's all good!"

I immediately felt an overwhelming peace come over me. Even though my human self felt small and helpless, the biggest part of me, which I refer to as my "spiritual self", began to emerge and take control. I calmly sat back in my high backed chair and closed my eyes.

The darkest night shows the brightest stars. I have learned that the darker things seem, the brighter the blessing at hand. "Hit me with your best shot. Bring it on!" I exclaimed. I completely surrendered my trust to the wisdom of a most loving God, and began to brace myself for the outcome. I knew that whatever would happen from this point on was for the *greater good*. Knowing this eliminated my fear and I began to feel empowered. I had all the loving energy of the universe on my side, and I felt strong and light with peace.

I called on the trillions of galaxies of the universe, and instructed the powerful *Love Force* of God to beam down on my child. In my mind, I could see a brilliant, shimmering light illuminating her body, where she lay on the hospital bed. I envisioned the Divine Mother glowing in the golden light and asked her to take charge. Then I saw the loving Master, Jesus, holding Denise in his arms with the most awesome tenderness, rocking her and healing her with *Love*.

At 5 p.m. it was visiting hour again. As her father and I walked into the Critical Care Unit to bed number one, I could hear the music from my piano, quietly filling Denise's room. I had instructed the nurses to keep pressing play on the CD player so she could hear my recordings on *The Quiet Journey* CD that she was so familiar with. It gave me great comfort to know that somehow in her coma, Denise would be able to hear her Mommy's music and know that I was spiritually with her.

Denise's vital signs were still very critical and she had developed pneumonia. The nurse told us that she had moved her leg earlier and when she said it, I could hear a trace of optimism in her voice. As I stared at my sweet daughter, lying in a lifeless coma my thoughts were only of my complete love for her. I silently thanked her for choosing me to be her mother and as I bent down to kiss her cheek, I asked her to, "Please return to us."

Her Daddy reached down to kiss her cheek and as he did, I saw her eyelash flutter ever so slightly. It was in that moment that I knew she was on her way back. I could feel her teetering between "here" and "there" in a place only a chosen few witness in a lifetime. I also knew that she was in a beautiful, peaceful place and coming back to us would not be easy.

At 3 a.m. the night nurse, Amy, woke me up in the waiting room and told me Denise wanted to see me. My baby was awake! She had come back to us and was on her way to recovery.

The next day I learned that Denise did go to the peaceful place. As she weakly spoke of her mystical journey, she seemed transformed. She was filled with beautiful wisdom. I was in complete awe of the saintly words flowing from her mouth. Denise had seen what she refers to as "A golden light outlined with a deep blue." I asked her, "Is there a reason we are here?" She answered, "Yes Mommy. We are here to experience life. It comes with both pain and happiness."

Denise revealed to me that she tried to go into the tunnel of light, but *they* wouldn't let her in. She said *they* kept saying, "*Go* to your *Mommy*." Later she told me, "If it's not your time, it's not your time and *they* send you back."

Denise says that the loving, golden light of God is everywhere. "People just can't see it. I can... if I close my eyes I can see the light anytime I want. Now I know the big picture." As she spoke of her near death experience I thought, "What an honor it is to be your mother!"

Life is an adventure that we choose at the soulful level. It is our contract with God. All of us have a divine purpose and all of us are equally important. Life is about rediscovering *who we are*. We are all students and we are all teachers. My children have been my greatest teachers.

My journey in this lifetime has been experienced as a musician/composer. My purpose is to assist in awakening the spirit with music. I perform my compositions from a place I refer to as the *Source of Love*. Denise told me later that she could hear my piano recordings from "the other side". She said that hearing the music, gave her a path back to life and she could hear it playing as she regained consciousness.

This incident with my daughter occurred after *Butterfly Moments* was written. It was from the lessons that I am about to share with you that I was able to witness the whole event, of almost losing my precious daughter, with my spiritual eyes. I replaced my fear with God. I replaced my fear with *Love*.

Have you ever felt like God was speaking to you and just when you thought it might be your imagination, a butterfly lands on your shoulder and *will not leave*?? This happened to me three different times inside of an enlightening week I shall never forget! The story of the butterfly is amazing and will be explained in detail later in the book. As a result of that awesome experience, I now refer to those magical moments that make the soul sing and the body shudder with emotion, *Butterfly Moments*.

Each one of us has a divine purpose. We are *never* alone. I repeat...*we are never alone!* A small, delicate, orange and black butterfly taught me this lesson on a beautiful September morning, while I was having an inquisitive conversation with God. This was a major turning point in my awareness of the divine that dwells within all of us. I began to recognize that *Butterfly Moments* happen every day. I hope that in sharing what I have come to know, you will better recognize these quiet, beautiful moments that occur everyday in your life. My story was written for *you* with *Love*.

Me, Myself and I

"What's in a name?
That which we call a rose
by any other name would smell as sweet."
—William Shakespeare
(Romeo and Juliet)

How many roles do you perform in your life? Do you find that your personality changes with each role? If you are like me, the number is endless. I have found that by naming them all, I do a much better job of keeping track of myself. I have labeled this process "Controlling My Natural Schizophrenia."

I first became aware that there was much more to me than just "one person" when I had my first child. Maybe you can relate. Picture this: you have planned a beautiful, romantic dinner for yourself and your lover. The cuisine is Italian this evening and a fine red wine accompanies the delicious meal that you have prepared.

The black lace you are wearing is for his eyes only. In fact it reveals so much of you that you would surely have to throw something else over it to answer the door. Oh yes, this is going to be an incredible and memorable evening!

From the window there is a beautiful view of a full moon nestled in a blanket of softly illuminated clouds. A warm, soft glow from a cozy, crackling fire fills the room and there is beautiful music playing quietly on the stereo. The special, fragrant candles you purchased to enhance sexual desire are filling the room with the aromas of sandalwood and musk.

You have prepared an after-dinner cordial for the two of you and the chemistry of human passion is beginning to ignite. Significant parts of your body are becoming warm and your eyes are locked into a loving gaze as his manly smell, coupled with his exquisite cologne, fills you with an incredible longing to nibble his neck.

He moves in slowly for that delicious first kiss. You are entering the climactic part of the evening. It is the magic beginning of this beautiful, romantic interlude. Closer... closer... Oh boy!... here we go... Closer... Closer.... Closer... and then!... and then! YES!!!! the baby cries.

Now there are two of you having a conversation in your head. The *Mother* has shown up, attempting to take over the whole program. She is putting quite a kink in your romantic evening.

"Pick up the baby."

"No, she'll stop crying in a minute."

"But she's gone from fussing to really crying! She needs to be fed and probably changed."

"What about my dinner... the music... the candles... he smells so good! Everything is so perfect."

Sadly enough, if you are a conscientious mother, the baby is going to win.

Having this awareness has worked very well for me in the entertainment business. As a musician, songwriter and composer I do three different genres of music. It only made sense that I name all three of the different songwriter/composers inhabiting my body.

I started my career singing my *Jose Cuervo* song as *Cindy Jordan* in bars and honkytonks all over Southern California. I used this as my stage name and since I was in my second marriage it seemed that using my maiden name was the safest way to go.

Cindy Jordan was the name I used in media and public performances. She is a girl who loves to "party" and have a good time! She loves to drink little shots of tequila and flirt with good-looking cowboys.

After *Jose Cuervo* became a hit, I moved to Texas with my new cowboy husband. When I told Dennis that I would like to have more children he was gracious enough to oblige my request and he did so, very eloquently. As I recall, his exact words were, "Woman...If you can be bred, I'm a gonna breed ya!" We became pregnant with Denise on our honeymoon.

Now that my tummy was full of baby, honkytonks didn't seem appropriate anymore. I had gone from tight-fittin' jeans to elastic and my attitudes and priorities had also made a shift. I found myself thinking it would be a good idea to go back to church.

The first day I walked into St. Lawrence of Brindisi in Waskom, Texas, I saw an old upright piano that I soon found out was badly in need of tuning. During the service, I was very aware that the congregation was making a good-hearted attempt at having music in the church but it was pretty sad. No one was playing the piano.

Afterwards, several people came up to our family and introduced themselves (Texans are so friendly). I walked over to the piano and began to tinker on it to see if it was in tune. I asked them if they needed someone to play for them.

"O my goodness!! Thank God!" exclaimed Lori Hughes. Several of them got excited and started saying things like, "You are the answer to our prayers!" "You are an angel sent by God!" This is a miracle!"

In my mind *Cindy Jordan* was saying, "Wait! Hold it!! You don't understand!! I wrote *Jose Cuervo*. You know, that song about a girl who can only open one eye and she has a hangover because she drank so much tequila that she can't remember what she did the night before. Yeah, the song where she wakes up next to a cowboy she doesn't recognize and she's wearing his shirt."

I just kept my thoughts silent and showed up the next Sunday and just about every Sunday after that for 12 years.

It seemed that the most natural thing to do at this point was to write children's Christian music. The first song I wrote was *When You Walk With The Lord* and I taught it to the children at church. This evolved into 3 albums and a children's choir with 35 members we called *Kids for Kids*.

One Sunday, one of the children's grandmothers made the comment, "How can a woman who writes a song about whiskey write songs about God!" When this came back to me I realized that her honest question had a valid point so I created *Miss Cindy*. I patterned her after Mary Poppins and I began telling people I went from JC to JC (Jose Cuervo to Jesus Christ).

In 1997, I discovered there was still *another* musical composer inhabiting my body. She was very different from *Miss Cindy* and *Cindy Jordan*.

I named her *Cynthia*. Cynthia was trained as a classical pianist who writes piano music from the deep passions of her soul. She is graceful, elegant, and very wise.

Cindy Jordan, Miss Cindy and *Cynthia* are very different from each other. Each has her own unique personality and individual style of music. They even dress differently. My husband, Dennis, says it's like being married to three different women.

I find it be very exciting to think that we can create new dimensions of ourselves anytime. I know that somewhere inside of me there is a *Mother, Wife, Lover, Little Girl, Teenager, Sister, Niece, Aunt, Granddaughter, Confidante, Friend, Country Songwriter, Children Songwriter, Composer, Author, Real Stinker, Flaky Broad, Surfer, Seeker, Student, Teacher, Domestic Goddess, Music Goddess, Goddess of Love, Warrior Princess, Doer, Leader, Procrastinator,* and an *Athlete* all inhabiting the same body. The list is endless.

I have had a lot of fun with it. I used to have a manager who was aware of this little name game I played with myself. Royce is a funny guy. He used to say, "I'd like y'all to call a meeting and elect a spokesperson that can represent y'all. Then you can give me a report." I named the spokesperson Cindy Lou.

Some of my personalities I like better than others and I have mentally put duct tape over the mouths of the ones I don't much care for. I keep them quiet and put away in a safe place. They include the *Nag*, the *Victim* and the *Gossip*. I use them to remind me of what I *don't* want to be. These are the ones I have to forgive and work on because they bring negativity and "dis-ease" to the whole.

Recently, I had an experience with a group of speakers that brought all of this to light. We had been at a workshop and the guest speaker, Mark Le Blanc was sitting at our lunch table. I gave him one of my CDs.

After giving Mark a music CD he asked if I had a business card. I reached in my purse and to my delight I saw that I had remembered my card case. However I had forgotten that I had put blanks in there. Without looking I smiled as I handed him a *blank card!*

He turned it over several times and looked at me with a kind of puzzled look on his face. "Oops," I said very innocently. Everyone, including me, burst out laughing.

Being the very gracious man that he is, Mark quietly said, "This is great! I am going to use this when I speak." Trying to make light of it I quickly said, "That's right! You can tell everyone that a "blonde" in Nashville, Tennessee, gave you a blank business card when you asked for her contact information." As it turned out, it was really quite brilliant.

Mark saw it first. He said he would never forget me. How many business cards do we get that we can't remember where or why we got them? I get so many that I have to make notes on them or I completely forget who gave it to me.

I suddenly realized that the blank card was like Deepak Chopra's, "field of full potentiality". In other words, there was no limit to who I could be on that card. I could write Miss Cindy, Cynthia, Cindy Jordan or any name and identity for that matter! I realized at that moment that there is no limit to who *I am*.

I think that the hardest thing in life is knowing *what it is you want to be when you grow up*. When you finally know, it is a triumphant epiphany. From that moment on you can create the person you want to be.

Simply create a list of all the characteristics and accomplishments you aspire to become, and be "that". Don't miss the scenery on your road to get there. This is your *Yellow Brick Road* and it is full of wonderful adventures. Be patient with yourself and forgive yourself when those negative personalities creep in. Just gently dismiss them and move on. Remember every moment is a new beginning.

There are no limits to who you can create yourself to be. This is because you always have free access to the *God Energy* inside of you. The great Master, Jesus said, "You can do all these things and much greater things than I."

Make that person you create someone you respect and love with your heart and soul. The Lady Cynthia, is my masterpiece and I work on her daily. She is beautiful, wise, elegant, powerful, and ageless. Lady Cynthia uses the power of *Love* to manifest and create miracles in her life.

This book is the story of my journey to enlightenment. I hope it gives you insight as you progress on yours.

Bright Blessings!!
Cynthia

Cindy Jordan

A Musical Childhood

"Thou hath no youth or age"
—Shakespeare
1564–1616
(Measure for Measure)

I was born Cynthia Louise Jordan on the fourth of May, 1954, in Long Beach, California, at 2:42 p.m. The sun was in Taurus, the moon was in Gemini and Virgo was rising. This was the magical moment of birth God chose to present me to the world and to my wonderful parents Duke and Margie Jordan.

The universe decided that I would come into this lifetime as a female. For the last nine months or so, after a delightful encounter between my parents, I was alive! From that magical moment of conception, God had been busily working on my tiny new form and my soul was joyfully rejoicing the fact that it had a new residence.

I am a miracle. My mother never had to worry about making my heart, or my lungs or my ten fingers and toes. All she had to do was eat right and get plenty of rest. All Daddy had to do was satisfy Mom's unending craving for A&W Root Beer. God took care of the rest.

Upon entry, I had a little trouble breathing and spent my first three days in an oxygen tent. My grandfather, Albert Solis put on his best suit to visit me. From what I hear, this was quite a big deal. Upon seeing me, he told my grandmother, Tita, "One day those tiny little fingers are going to play the piano." Somehow it seemed that, even then, he was aware of my destiny. I was his first grandchild and I later named him Papu (Pop-oo). Although he passed away when I was only six years old he is always with me.

I grew up in Redondo Beach, California, just three blocks from the ocean. I attended Catholic School for twelve years. Yes folks… I wore the uniform and studied with the Franciscan order. I shared that time with three younger brothers whom I love dearly. Steve, Mark and Kurt are still like best friends. I guess I will always have that "big sister" attitude and there is nothing I wouldn't do for any of them.

My mother's family is of Spanish descent and my father's family is Scots-Irish. I like to think that I inherited the fiery Latin and Celtic passions from the two sides. My mother's maiden name was Margarita Estella Solis and my father is Roland Henry Jordan, but everyone calls him "Duke." I am very proud of my heritage and I was greatly influenced with musical talents on both my mother and father's sides of the family.

Spanish was the first language my mother knew. My grandmother wanted me to call her "Abuelita", but I called her "Tita", and the name stuck. Tita was born in the city of Parral, Chihuahua, located in Northern Mexico. I loved to hear her stories of meeting the "ruthless and terrible" Pancho Villa when she was only three years old. "Villa" as Tita called him, stole the beautiful family villa and used it for his headquarters.

Pancho Villa kidnapped Tita's father and oldest brother and held them for ransom. My great grandmother, "Mama Tita," collected two ransoms. The first had been stolen by one of Villa's guards. After they were finally released, the family moved to El Paso, Texas. It was there that Tita married her "love," Albert Solis (my Papu).

Papu's father, Albert Senior, was a talent scout for Irving Berlin. He traveled all around the world looking for Spanish Music and was actually searching for songs in Spain during the Spanish Revolution. My mother remembers him saying, "We had to dodge bullets during the day and close the shutters at night." He also worked for RCA Victor talking machines. We called him Papa and he was godfather to both my mother and me. I remember he loved to watch the bull fights on Saturday night TV.

Daddy was born at home. The house was located on the Universal Studio lots in Southern California. His birth certificate actually says "Universal City," which is where my grandfather, "Sport", tended the horses and worked as an extra in some of the early western movies.

Sport was a real cowboy. My dad remembers that they used to have rodeos on the lots and drink "bathtub beer." We lost my grandfather in WWII while he was held prisoner on a Japanese prison ship where he was subjected to horrific conditions for over three years. We have a letter from another soldier who was in the same prison camp. In it he tells us that my grandfather sang in the prison camp to help with the morale of his fellow Americans. He received a Purple Heart, which is given to soldiers who are wounded in action. He was also given the Silver Star for his incredible bravery. This was presented to his widow, my grandmother, "Moe".

Moe had never worked before. For the first time she found herself the sole support of the family. She ran a milling machine at a defense plant during the day and at night she played honky-tonk piano to support her four children. Moe had amazing energy and she could really WOW! an audience. I once saw her play the piano and sing for two hours without stopping. When she finally tried to take a break, the audience wouldn't let her stop.

Her fans called her "The last of the red hot Mamas!" Every Sunday morning, after church, we went to Moe's house for pancakes. After breakfast I would beg her to play. When I was very small she would let me reach up and play the high keys on the piano as she belted out songs like *Bill Bailey* and *Shanty Town*. She was a great entertainer!

I can recall my first spiritual music memory, which happened when I was just a toddler. I was very small when I first heard the melody to *Greensleeves*. For some reason the music seemed to be like a familiar old friend. From that day, every time I hear *Greensleeves* I have an emotional pause that fills my heart with quiet passion. Even though I was very young, the soul is ageless and the memory is profound. It can be a beautiful *Butterfly Moment* when music gives us a sense of timelessness and immortality.

When I was three years old, Santa Claus brought me my first piano. It looked like a miniature red grand piano and it even had a little red bench. My mother taught me to play *Chop Sticks*. It was the first song I learned to play.

There was always music in the house. My parents both sing and my mother woke us up every morning with a song. When I was about seven years old I learned how to play by ear on a Magnus chord organ. I begged and I begged for lessons and finally on June 1, 1964, I had my first piano lesson.

    I will never forget that day. I was dancing around in our backyard with excitement waiting for my 4 o'clock lesson. We didn't own a piano so our good friends and neighbors, Beth and Wally Skiba, were gracious enough to let me practice on theirs. No one ever had to tell me to practice and Cuddles, the dog, greeted me at their fence everyday. I can still remember the smell of their home. I was making music and I loved it!

    On May 4, 1965 Tita gave me a piano for my eleventh birthday. I had never seen anything so beautiful! It was a shiny black upright and it had a lovely tone. Popu had passed away five years earlier. Tita told me that she had bought me the piano because he always wanted to see "those little fingers play."

    My piano teacher's name was Mrs. Lopez and we became great friends. One day when I was twelve years old she sat me down and said, "I can't teach you anymore. When you came to me you were like a sponge but we have gone as far as we can go."

    She brought me to a man who would change my life in music forever. Dr. Nino Albanese was a gentle Italian man who had played piano concerts all over the world. He wasn't very tall in stature but to me he was magnificent! He showed me a whole new world of music and I soon found out that I had much to learn. Dr. Albanese was my greatest teacher and I can feel his spirit with me every time I practice or perform. It is as if he has his hands on my shoulders guiding me along.

    I remember one day when I went for a lesson and I couldn't get it together. After it was clear I wasn't concentrating very well, he finally said, "Let's take a walk." We went to his garden where he had built a pond full of giant goldfish. He said, "I am your teacher, but it doesn't always have to be music." Just recently, I visited his widow and I was honored when she gave me his favorite book, *Cosmic Consciousness* by Richard Maurice Bucke. Even now I feel like I am still learning from him.

    I taught myself to play the guitar and when I was seventeen I decided I wanted to teach music lessons. My dad to this day will tell you he didn't think I could pull it off. When Daddy asked me if I felt qualified enough to teach, I simply told him, "All you have to do to be a teacher is to know more than your student." I wanted to make learning fun and I ended up with about twenty guitar and piano students. I really enjoy teaching music.

Being the true Baby Boomer that I am, I love Rock and Roll. I woke up every morning to music and fell asleep to it every night. Whenever I had the opportunity I would listen to KHJ or KRLA through the small earphone that streamed up from my transistor radio, which I had hidden inside my school desk. I was brought up with Elvis Presley, the Beatles and the Rolling Stones. I loved it all!

There are events that happen in our lifetime that have such an impact that we remember vividly where we were and what we were doing at the time they happened. I was in the third grade, on the St. Lawrence Martyr School playground, when my friend Pauline Short told me President Kennedy had been shot. We were wearing our red plaid uniforms, white blouses with a Peter Pan collar, bobby socks and oxfords. I remember Pauline had tears streaming down her freckled cheeks and I was completely stunned with disbelief. It was a horrible feeling of violation and it penetrated deep within the soul. Even now I can vividly remember the experience.

We were at our friends, the Weltons, the day I first saw John, Paul, George and Ringo sing *I Wanna Hold Your Hand* on the Ed Sullivan Show. I remember the adults making comments about the Beatles' "shaggy long hair." I was 10 years old and I was hooked!

The Beatles as a group and as individuals have been a great influence on my musical career. As their lives evolved and they became more spiritually aware, so did their music. I understand this because the *exact* same thing happened to me. Music is the expression of the soul and those of us who create the music, tend to expose our secret selves.

Throughout the Beatles' career, their music changed right along with the generation that loved them so. When they first appeared on the scene in 1964, they had a unique rock and roll sound that appealed to young pre-teens like me. As we all matured, so did their music.

The songwriting talents of Lennon and McCartney became beautifully poetic in their album *Rubber Soul*. *Magical Mystery Tour* is full of imagination and symbolic metaphor. Psychedelic drugs and imagination were woven throughout the lyrics of the classic albums *Sergeant Pepper Lonely Hearts Club Band* and *Abbey Road*. The Beatles' music clearly describes the characteristics of the baby-boomer generation of which I am proudly a member.

The *White Album* is a timeless masterpiece. The songs *Revolution* and *Helter Skelter* expressed the emotions of rage and confusion associated with the Vietnam War. At that time, peace and free love were the themes of the young people in America. Our friends and brothers were being drafted and killed in a war that seemed senseless. After going through *hell* in Vietnam our soldiers would come home to war protesters who would spit at them and call them "baby killers". The emotional climate in our country concerning the Vietnam War was insanely chaotic. The Beatles described it well in their music.

When George Harrison introduced the group to the spiritual world of India, their music became a beautiful expression of "Peace and Love". John Lennon became politically involved in America and wrote songs like *All You Need Is Love* and *Imagine*. Young people all over the world were chanting, "All we are saying is give peace a chance." George Harrison brought awareness to poverty and world hunger when he did his famous concert for Bangladesh. I have realized much about my own spiritual growth through the changing music of the Beatles. They have been wonderful teachers in my life.

There are no accidents. All of our lessons are the same. We have all learned about love, betrayal, trust, courage, fear, friendship, giving and receiving in different ways. It is only the characters and the dramas that are different. As I tell my story I realize that everything that I learned in my childhood prepared me for my mission in life. It was a perfect plan created by God just for me. Your childhood was perfectly designed just for you as well.

The hardest thing in life is to know what it is you want to be when you grow up. When you finally discover your purpose it is a grand epiphany! The future had many unexpected surprises in store for this surfer girl and making music would be the theme of my Journey as I headed down my very own *Yellow Brick Road*. Little did I know that I would one day write a hit song that some people still refer to as "The Party Song of the 80s!"

IN MY LIFE
—John Lennon and Paul McCartney

There are places I'll remember
All my life though some have changed
Some forever not for better
Some have gone and some remain

All these places had their moments
With lovers and friends I still can recall
Some are dead and some are living
In my life, I've loved them all

But of all these friends and lovers
There is no one compares with you
And these memories lose their meaning
When I think of love as something new

Though I know I'll never lose affection
For people and things that went before
I know I'll often stop and think about them
In my life, I'll love you more

Through A Child's Eyes

*"The kingdom of the Father
is spread out upon the earth
and people do not see it"*
—Jesus of Nazareth
Book of Thomas

We are all loving spirits discovering ourselves through the human experience. The purpose of *Life* is for us to remember who we really are and realize our true nature, which is *love*. I have learned to see the world through the eyes of my children. It is through their experiences that I have my own.

Some of my favorite memories are those times I took my children to Disneyland. We have some great video footage of my daughter Julie riding on Dumbo and in the seat next to her, with a great big smile on his face, sits a big man, my Dad. Julie calls her grandfather Papa and he stands 6 feet and 4 inches tall. It is quite a sight to watch the two of them going round and round and up and down on Dumbo. They are both smiling and laughing and waving as they go by. The picture is full of love and it fills my heart every time I see it.

When we take a child to Disneyland, our experience depends on their experience. If they have a good time, we have a good time. If the child is fussing and complaining, Disneyland, with all of its magic and imagination, is no fun at all.

Just as we have the Disneyland experience through the eyes of a child, God has the human experience through us. We are his children and when we enjoy life, God enjoys life.

God is Love. Therefore when we experience Love we experience God. I like to call God, *Love*. It makes it easier for me to know and understand God. Through our experience God enjoys the human experience of Love. It's a beautiful exchange.

I think of it in the following way:

In the beginning there was God and only God. God is *Love*.

Therefore, in the beginning there was *Love* and only *Love*. *Love* wanted to experience itself so *Love* decided that it would create a being that would have the capability to feel love, make love, and know love.

Love was invisible and decided this being would have a physical form. *Love* called this new creation a human. *Love* would inhabit the human form and silently just "be". The *human being* would possess a spirit, a heart, and intellect, which would enable it to rationalize and experience all kinds of different emotions. Through these emotions *Love* would have the *human love experience*.

Love had some great ideas and was very excited. It wanted the human to be happy and enjoy the beautiful gift of life. *Love* designed and created a beautiful world, which the human would call "home". There were deep blue oceans, grand mountains, scenic deserts and lush valleys. *Love* then created colorful flowers, and beautiful plants and trees to decorate the landscape.

After the "home" was finished *Love* created all kinds of wonderful animals to share this magnificent new world. The animals each had different lessons to teach the human and they would all live together in harmony. This wonderful new existence was like a great big Disneyland. It was the most beautiful, magical place in the universe. *Love* called it Heaven!

There would be a male and female form with a few differences between them. The male body would hold the seed to reproduce more humans. The female body would receive the seed inside her womb where little baby humans would grow inside her body. More baby humans gave *Love* the opportunity to experience more life.

Love designed the act of planting the seed a beautiful way for the male and female to connect *as one* both physically and spiritually. It was designed to be very enjoyable and the human would come to call it "making Love". From this exciting union the human could discover and realize that it was created from *Love*.

In fact, the "making love" act was designed to be so enjoyable that unlike the animals (with the exception of dolphins) humans could *make love* without the intention to procreate. *Love* saw this as a beautiful gift to bring the female and male together. This would be a great way to express *Love* and at the same time satisfy the deep desire to feel complete. By *making love* humans could better understand *oneness*.

The man, woman and baby humans would live together as a family. The man would provide food and shelter. The woman would be the main heart center for the family to experience *Love*. The family would live in harmony with other families and they would all be happy in the beautiful world *Love* created just for their enjoyment.

There was one more thing. *Love* needed to create an opposite to know itself better. After all contrast is the best teacher. It needed a strong opposition based on fear so ego was created. Ego was made of fear and illusion.

Ego got its power by fooling the human into thinking that the value of the human was measured by the possession of things and a false sense of control. The ego also tricked the human into thinking there was a limited supply of everything, including *Love*. It would even misuse the beautiful act of *making love*.

Finally, the great day came and the plan was in action. It was time for *Love* to experience life in the human form. The human was created from *Love*, just as a flute is made from a tree. This would be remembered in magical moments of the human's life. *Love's* voice is silent, but the human would discover *Love* through the heart and soul where *Love* and the human are one.

Love could feel emotion and hear the human's thoughts. It could see, hear, taste, and smell all of the beautiful things that had been created. It could feel the rain, the warmth of a fire and a loving kiss.

Love was experiencing life! Before *Love* had only existed but now it was *alive!* Yes! *Love* was alive!

Little by little, the human started to become aware of *Love*. The human began to realize that there was some kind of Great Intelligence that had created the world and the stars and planets beyond. As the human became more aware it named *Love*, God. The humans have named the ego, Devil. It constantly challenges *Love* with trickery and false illusion. If it doesn't feel warm and fuzzy, it's not *Love*.

There have been a few humans who have known *Love* and have become great teachers. One of them was a man named Jesus. Since the beginning of Christianity, the world has argued whether or not Jesus was human or divine. Jesus said, "I am the Light." This is because he was enlightened and taught what he knew about *Love*. His very powerful message is full of truth and has sustained throughout the ages.

Enlightenment is simply discovering *we are Love*. When we know this and finally discover the power of love, *Love* is able to know itself. This is when we see Heaven on Earth or as Jesus said, "On earth as it is in heaven".

In the Book of Thomas, Jesus was asked, "Lord, where is the kingdom of heaven?" Jesus said, "The Kingdom of Heaven is on earth, man just cannot see it." Jesus knew.

Jesus taught that Love is the answer to everything. This message feels warm to the human soul because it is our soul that is one with God. The soul is the part of us that sees the earth as heaven. The essence of the soul is *Love*.

When we experience love, *Love* shines through our eyes like a bright light. Just like Papa riding Dumbo with little Julie Lynn, his experience of the love and laughter shared on the ride was a result of her experience. God is having the human experience through you. Are you showing God a good time?

Next time you pause at a beautiful sunset, be aware of that *silent observer* inside that is watching and loving you every moment of your life. In the past you might have said something like, "God, you are so AWESOME! Thank you for painting this beautiful sunset in the sky so I can be reminded that you are with me. It is a heavenly gift to be sure."

This time be quiet and listen for the silent voice of God. You might hear something like, "Thank you, (your name), for pausing to witness this beautiful sunset I created for you so that I could experience it through your eyes, your heart and *our* soul. Together we are witnessing heaven on earth." These are the times I know as *Butterfly Moments*.

WILLIAM WORDSWORTH
(FROM THE EXCURSION)
(1814)

I have seen
A curious child, who dwelt upon a tract
Of inland ground applying to his ear
The convolutions of a small lipped shell
To which, in silence hushed, his very soul
Listened intensely, and his countenance soon
Brightened with joy, for from within were heard
Murmurings, whereby the monitor expressed
Mysterious union with its native sea
Even such a shell the universe itself
Is to the ear of faith; and there are times
I doubt not, when to you it doth impart
Authentic tidings of invisible things;
Of ebb and flow, and ever-during power;
And central peace, subsisting at the heart
Of endless agitation

Be Kind to Your Waitress

"Weep no more, nor sigh, nor groan
Sorrow calls no time that's gone;
Violets plucked, the sweetest rain
Makes not fresh or grow again"
—John Fletcher
1579–1625
(The Queen of Corinth)

The universe has created a perfectly organized series of events to teach each of us the lessons we need to know at the time we need to know them. I don't think that anyone is a stranger. We are all just friends that haven't met…at least in this lifetime.

I heard a great metaphor once comparing each of our lives to a beautiful tapestry. From the bottom of the weaving loom where all of the colorful threads are hanging the pattern doesn't quite make sense. It can be very confusing and almost chaotic looking. From the top of the tapestry we can easily see a perfect picture. The Loving Creator has crafted an exquisite design especially for your life and it is highlighted with golden threads of love.

When we are finally aware that there is no such thing as a *coincidence*, life can get very exciting. You start looking at everyone as a potential teacher. Or maybe he or she is the student that benefits from something you do or say. There can be a beautiful exchange with any human being at any time. All you need to do is to focus on that *Love* energy that we all know and share.

Human Beings have a deep desire to be acknowledged for *being* alive. This is because somewhere deep inside we all know that we have a purpose. Everything really does happen for a reason. The fact you exist at all is a miracle in itself. A kind word or a smile can be a generous gift in somebody's day when we give with that part of us that is *Love*.

There are many people I have met and events that have taken place that have taught me valuable lessons. They are those magical intersections on Life's Journey that stay with us forever as a golden memory. One of these events instantly comes to mind.

It was the week before Christmas, 1975. My daughter, Julie, was three years old, and her daddy, Steve, and I had split up. Now it was Daddy's house and Mommy's house and she was confused. It was a very emotional time for all of us. She would cry when Steve would bring her home after visiting him. Divorce is horrible on children and there is a lot of pain when you see your children hurting. It just adds to the fact that you are hurting yourself.

I was working as a waitress in a very nice dinner house in Torrance, California, called Ichabod Crane's. They featured delicious prime rib dinners. It was fashioned after the 18th century novel, *The Legend of Sleepy Hollow*, by Nathaniel Hawthorne. The food waitresses dressed as Katrina with bonnets and full long skirts. The bartenders dressed in poet shirts and dark brown vests. I was a cocktail waitress and we dressed like the school master, Ichabod Crane. We wore black velvet knickers, a brocade vest that fit snuggly under our chest and a white under blouse with full, three quarter sleeves. I liked it because our uniform didn't reveal parts of us that didn't need to be revealed. It was a very nice place to work.

To enhance the scholastic theme of *Ichabod Crane*, the cocktail lounge was decorated as a library full of antiques and old books. On one side of the lounge there was a patio with lots of windows and French doors.

I am very private when I have emotional upsets in my life. I don't like to bring others down with my negativity and I do a pretty good job at covering up. This particular day I wasn't doing a very good job of it. I had completely dropped two trays of drinks, one of which had six Margaritas in long stemmed glasses. It was not what I would consider a "good day." Little did I realize it would be a great day that I would never forget!

This particular December afternoon a party of about eight people had come in to have a Christmas drink. There were three women and five men in their late twenties or early thirties and it was obvious to me that they probably worked in an office together.

I walked over to take their drink order. As I approached the table they were all smiling, joking around and obviously happy to be in a relaxed environment. I asked for their order and returned to my station. Sam was tending bar. He made their drinks and I brought them to the table. One man had ordered coffee so I went to the kitchen in the back to make a fresh pot. In the meantime unbeknownst to me, Sam had brought a fresh pot of coffee up to the front.

I collected the money for the drinks. Remember this was 1975 and drinks were $1.50. The bill was $12.75. We had small pink tip trays and I left my tray with their change on the table. When I came back to check on them there was nothing on the tip tray. A big fat zero! It was obvious that I was being "stiffed" which is restaurant talk for "no tip". They all watched me as I picked up the empty tray. This party of eight was giving me a silent message that was ringing loud and clear!

I felt a sinking feeling in my stomach. I was already sunk pretty low but this was just another blow on an already broken heart. I put the empty tip tray on my serving tray and started to walk away. All of a sudden with a big sigh I turned back around, held up the small pink tray for all to see and said to the people at the table, "Can somebody please tell me why my tip tray is empty?"

They couldn't believe it! I couldn't believe it! Did those words really come out of my mouth? It was like someone else was talking. Oh well, in for a penny, in for a pound. I repeated myself, "Can someone please tell me why this is empty?" I said still holding up the tray. You see, we are dependent on our tips because we are paid less than minimum wage. I need to know what I did wrong. Did everybody get their drinks OK? Did I miss something?"

For a moment, no one said a word. They just all looked at each other I guess wondering who would be their spokesperson. Some of them were even squirming around and the sly crooked smiles on the women were the easiest for me to understand.

Finally someone spoke up. "You were rude." Oh my gosh...me?? Rude?? I was shocked.

One woman said, "You didn't smile." What!! Me, not smile! You're kidding! I had no idea my sadness was showing through.

Then they were on me fiercely, like a pack of dogs. I think I was being used as an example as they criticized my lack of good PR and service to the customer. This was obviously something important to them in their business, and I was painfully aware that I had not been showing my best side.

One man said, "I had to get up and get my own coffee." I apologized to him and told him I was unaware that Sam had made coffee and had brought it to the front.

I thanked them for their honesty and as I started to walk away the man who had gotten his coffee threw one more stone. This was the fateful one that would surely break the camel's back. He smirked, looked at his colleagues and said, "And don't try to tell us you've had a BAD DAY." Then he kind of grunted a satisfied "humph".

That was it. I stood there a very long moment. I tried to restrain it but couldn't. It wasn't a trickle, or even a rain. It was a flood! Yep, the dam broke wide open and my tears were uncontrollable. I was sobbing and could hardly catch my breath as I profusely apologized to this poor unsuspecting party of eight.

"I... I... I... am... so... so... so... sorry if... I... I... ru... ru... ruined...your...Christmas, Christmas celebration!" I stuttered as I sobbed, making short panting breaths between each syllable. "I...I...I...had no...no...no idea! I HAVE had a terrible day! My life is horrible and I am very sad. But this is not YOUR fault!!" I put down my tray pointed to my eyes. "And these are not your fault!" I was sobbing between each word and my face was very wet. It was a welcome release. "Please accept my apology!! I had no idea!!"

Surprise, empathy and "I can't believe she had the nerve" would best describe the looks on their faces. They were all staring at me looking dumbfounded. I can still see the image of their catatonic faces with mouths opened wide as if they were about to get a big dose of cough medicine. It was a memorable picture that I shall never forget.

With that, I excused myself and went to the locker room where I had a wonderful, hard cleansing cry. I don't know how long I was in the room but I know it took quite a while to pull it back together.

When I finally returned to the lounge the party of eight was gone. The silence was deafening on the patio where they had been seated before. It was like walking on the set after a major dramatic scene in a movie.

I went to the table to clear it off but Sam, who knew I was upset, had cleared the glasses. There lying all by itself was a beautiful, green $10.00 bill. In 1975, a tip of $10.00 on a tab of $12.75 was very generous. It warmed my heart and I felt like I was getting a giant hug from eight strangers who had shared this incredible moment with me.

So...who were these people and did I ever see them again?

About two weeks later I was waiting on two men who had come in for Happy Hour. I was back to my happy-go-lucky persona, which was a more normal state of being for me. I remember my smile was especially big that day. One of the men told his friend with much excitement in his voice, "This is her!! This is her!!"

"Excuse me?" I asked.

"Remember I came in with some people from my office, and we sat at the patio and..."

"Oh yes," I replied, "I know exactly who you are!" It was then that I knew that the story had made it back to the office, to clients and probably friends and families of everyone who was there on that memorable December afternoon.

I had been the teacher, and the student. These eight people who had come in to celebrate a festive Christmas drink were my teachers and my students. Now I am sharing this lesson with you.

Since that day I have never seen a "rude" waitress, cashier or anyone in public service again. I only see real people with real issues living their lives. Now, if someone comes off as rude, I try to give that person the benefit of the doubt. I usually send a blessing from my spirit to theirs. I believe that when you give a spiritual hug to someone, his or her spirit can feel the love energy that emanates from your body.

Thanks to that wonderful gentleman who didn't want to hear that I was having a "bad day" I have a new attitude with seemingly rude people.

Sometimes I ask my standard, "How are you doing on a scale of one to ten?" This question basically says, "I don't need details but I am concerned."

One time a woman was treating me horribly and when I asked her this question she told me she had just been diagnosed with malignant breast cancer. You just never know what someone else is going through.

When we show compassion, we are doing what I refer to as "Doing the God Thing." It's what God would do and it ignites that part of us that is one with God, which is one with *Love*.

Showing kindness to a troubled "stranger" who is really just a friend in disguise, can become a memorable *Butterfly Moment* for both of you to cherish the rest of your life.

It was while working at Ichabod Crane's that I would write a fun little song called *Jose Cuervo*—you are a friend of mine! My *Yellow Brick Road* was about to lead me into a challenging adventure called "The Music Business."

JOSE CUERVO

"Jose Cuervo you are a friend of mine!"
—Cindy Jordan

There are two questions that I am always asked since *Jose Cuervo* became a hit Country Song. The first question is, "Did you really do all those things that you wrote about in that song?" My standard answer to this is "Of course not! At least not in one night."

The second question is, "How do you make a song a hit?" I used to say, "If I knew the answer to that question, I would have a hundred more hits." Now I say, "I followed the laws of the universe." I just didn't know at the time that this is exactly how it happened.

It was 3 o'clock in the morning, the bewitching hour known well to musicians and cocktail waitresses. I had finished my evening shift and I was waiting for my boyfriend, Jim, to come over after work. I had poured a small glass of tequila and I was listening to one of my favorite songwriters, Kris Kristofferson, singing *On a Sunday morning sidewalk, wishing Lord that I was stoned, for there's something in a Sunday makes a body feel alone.*

My guitar was leaning against the sofa inviting me to play along. I picked her up and started singing my own set of words. It's Sunday morning and the sun is shining in my eye that is open and my head is spinning. I look at my feet and I still got both my boots on, I had too much tequila last night. Just one eye opens after too much tequila. On the coffee table sat my little glass of "Cuervo" and after taking a sip I sang: *Jose Cuervo, you are a friend of mine!* Then I tried to think of something that would rhyme. *I like to drink you with a little salt and lime.* "Hey, that's pretty good," I thought. *Did I kiss all the cowgirls did I shoot out the lights? Did I dance on the bar did I get in a fight.* I grabbed a pencil and wrote down the words that I had just sung. I was giving birth to my first "song child"!

A new idea was coming just as quickly as the first. *Now wait a minute things don't look too familiar. Who is this lady who's sleepin' beside me? She's awfully pretty but how'd she get my shirt on? I had too much tequila last night!* The whole birthing process took about fifteen minutes. Jim showed up and I sang him the first song I ever wrote and he thought it was great.

At the time I wrote *Jose Cuervo,* I was twenty-two years old and had already gone through a divorce. I had a beautiful little daughter, Julie Lynn, and we were more or less on our own. I was working as a cocktail waitress at Ichabod Crane's in Torrance, California, and I was making extra money on the side doing promotional work for Heublein. They are the major distributors for Jose Cuervo Tequila in the United States. I was paid $50 to wear a bikini at the beach and serve tequila to Heublein executives. I walked around volleyball tournaments with a sash that read "Miss Jose Cuervo." I guess this made me a human billboard. I saw it as getting paid for going to the beach and at the time it seemed like a great gig!

I decided to make a music demo of my song and show it to some of the marketing people in the company. The original version was written for a man to sing. I thought the lyrics were way too racy for a woman. I ended up with two versions of the song. I presented the song to Heublein but they didn't pay much attention to it.

I had heard about a talent contest at the KLAC country radio station in Los Angeles and submitted my song there. Somehow I got in the finals! The panel of judges was a quite impressive entourage of people in the music business. It included: Al Gallico, a big time publisher in Country Music; Snuff Garrett, who at the time was the music director for Clint Eastwood Movies; and Jack Lamier and Craig Applequist who were both in Promotions for what we know now as Sony Records. Al Gallico called me the day after the contest and asked to sign the song in his publishing company because everyone there had really liked it.

The talent contest was held at Magic Mountain. I had never sung in public before. I didn't know what a music chart was and I kept putting the microphone in front of the monitors. This was producing a very loud screeching noise that was extremely annoying.

I was 26 years old, wearing white hip hugger lace-up jeans, a cowboy hat and a white halter-top. I figured if I looked good enough maybe they wouldn't notice that I didn't know what I was doing. Needless to say, I lost the contest...big time! I called the station program director, Don Langford, and thanked him anyway. Somehow I knew, for reasons that I can't explain, that I wanted him to remember me.

In the meantime, Al Gallico had taken my *Jose Cuervo* demo to Nashville, Tennessee where it was turned down by everyone who heard it and with not much sugar coating I might add. I found out later that the general comment was "That's the biggest piece of &%!#! I ever heard!"

Al was too much of a gentleman to tell me this. I had known nothing about the music business but I was getting a crash course on how the whole thing works. All I knew was that every time I played and sang my little *Jose Cuervo* song, people loved it!

Since everyone in Nashville had "passed," I decided to record the song myself. My friend George Anderson who worked at KMPC radio agreed to pay for the recording. He brought in his friend, Alex, as a partner.

Alex had just won great recognition for his journalism in covering the hostage story in Iran. Somehow he was able to sneak in and convince the guards to allow him to communicate with the American prisoners. I remember he told me that he had a great technique for bribing the Arab soldiers. It seems that they loved peanut butter and jelly sandwiches!

I went to Quanta Studios to see about my recording session and it was there that I met a real character who called himself "Uncle Billy." He was full of exaggerated stories about people he knew in the music business. At that time I believed anything.

Uncle Billy introduced me to Denny Belfield to produce and arrange my song and we were on our way. Denny quickened the tempo and gave the song a signature "lick". This is music talk for that series of notes that give a song its identity. He hired all of the musicians including John Hobbs who played the piano. After just one take the track was all there. It had a really good *feel* and the musicians played it again "just because". It was like magic and after the second take the guitar player affirmatively exclaimed, "It's a hit!"

I took my new recording all pressed and finished back to Al Gallico.

He told me to take it to Larry Scott, who was a friend of his. Larry did the late night trucking show on KLAC from midnight to 6 a.m. I took my 45 to Larry and, as I was driving home from the station, he played it! I don't think any recording artist ever forgets that first time they hear themselves on the radio. It's as memorable as your first real kiss. *Jose Cuervo you are a friend of mine* was blasting over the airwaves and I was thrilled. It was almost beyond my comprehension to think that my song was actually being heard by thousands of people I didn't even know! It literally took my breath away.

Larry later told me that before the song was finished, "The phone lines lit up straight across just like it was Christmas!" It felt like Christmas to me! From that first night Larry said he would get requests for it every night and sometimes he would even play it more than once. I was officially in the music business.

Getting *Jose Cuervo* played in prime time was another story. Larry had a lot more freedom in those wee hours of the morning to play what he and the country fans liked. The morning traffic hours have the most listeners. Sponsors and music politics are in control of these prime hours between 6 and 9 a.m.

I called the program director, Don Langford, to tell him about my song. He remembered me from the talent contest. He told me it was the first time he had ever heard "Thank You" from someone who lost. I promised him an interview with Alex who happened to be very hot in the media because the hostages had just been set free. Don was happy to do it.

My friend George, Alex and I all showed up for the interview on the Sammy Jackson Morning Show and after the interview Sammy played *Jose Cuervo*. Sammy played the song almost every morning after that. I thought he was just being nice, but, afterwards, he told me that the reason he played it was because every time he did, he was "a hero" to his fans. Just as Larry experienced, people called in requesting the song.

There was a problem. The people didn't know where to buy *Jose Cuervo* and the station told me that without distribution they couldn't play it anymore. I took records to every record store I could in the Los Angeles area just to get them in stock. Then something amazing happened!

It had been several weeks since *Jose Cuervo* had first been heard on Larry Scott's Trucking Show. Al gave me a call. "Andy Wickham heard your song on KLAC and he wants to sign you on to Warner Brothers Records!" Whew! I was learning this goofy business as I went along, trying to keep up and stay with the flow. Apparently Mr. Wickham had been driving at around 3 a.m. after some kind of celebration and heard the song on Larry's show.

Warner Brothers, the "Bugs Bunny" people, bought the recording from George and sent me on a small promotional trip to Texas. It was there I met the head of promotions, Stan Byrd. I felt like Cinderella who had gone to the ball!

I flew first class for the first time in my life and I received the royal, red carpet treatment. But just like Cinderella, when the clock struck twelve, it all disappeared. Stan dropped my record and my phone calls went unanswered. I did everything I possibly could to keep things alive.

I created a line dance I called the Tequila Shuffle and taught it in clubs everywhere. I sang anywhere I could, including Chili Cook Offs and backyard parties. I was a has-been that never-was! My song never even placed on the national charts but somehow found its way to the number one spot in Los Angeles. This made no sense to me since Los Angeles, I was told, was the hardest market to break. I was well enough known locally, but my big dreams with Warner Brothers were over.

One afternoon in my living room I finally reached my limit. I had worked as hard as anyone could on my *Jose Cuervo* song and on top of that my personal life was in shambles. I was frustrated and angry and I had an ATTITUDE!

I found myself actually challenging God! "YOU DO IT!" I screamed. "I HAVE DONE ALL THAT I CAN DO! You made oceans and mountains and solar systems. IF YOU'RE EVEN LISTENING...YOU DO IT!" It had been a while since I had gone to church so I guess I figured that my "spiritual" membership had expired.

With that, I fell on my knees and sobbed a well-deserved cry. I didn't quit, I just knew I had done all I could do. I remember this emotional moment of surrender as if it just happened. It would turn out to be the most beautiful *Butterfly Moment* of my life although I wouldn't realize this for a long, long time. Little did I know that I had planted a beautiful garden that was just about ready to blossom.

Jose Cuervo
—Cindy Jordan

Well it's Sunday morning and the sun is shining
In my eye that is opened and my head is spinning
Was the life of the party and I can't stop grinnin'
I had too much tequila last night

Jose Cuervo you are a friend of mine
I like to treat you with a little salt and lime
Did I kiss all the cowboys? Did I shoot out the lights?
Did I dance on the bar? Did I start any fights?

Now wait a minute things don't look to familiar
And who is this cowboy who's sleeping beside me
He's kinda cute but how'd I get his shirt on
I had too much tequila last night

Jose Cuervo you are a friend of mine
I like to treat you with a little salt and lime
Did I kiss all the cowboys? Did I shoot out the lights?
Did I dance on the bar? Did I start any fights?

All those little shooters how I love to drink them down
C'mon bartender! Let's have another round
Well the music is playing and my spirits are high
Tomorrow might be painful but tonight we're gonna fly! High!

Jose Cuervo you are a friend of mine
I like to treat you with a little salt and lime
Every time we get together I sure have a good time
You're my friend you're the best
Mi amigo Cuervo

Jose Cuervo you are a friend of mine
I like to treat you with a little salt and lime
Did I kiss all the cowboys? Did I shoot out the lights?
Did I dance on the bar? Did I start any fights?

After the Surrender

"Love conquers all things;
let us surrender to love"
—Virgil
70–19 BC
(Eclogues)

When the farmer plants his crops his job is to work the land and plant the seed. After the farmer plants the seed he surrenders the rest to Mother Nature. There is a perfectly organized plan where all creation dances in harmony. It is a dance between the earth, sun and the rain that nourishes the seed. If the farmer were to pull on the small sprouts to hasten their growth he would destroy the crop. This is faith. The farmer does all he can do and then he lets God take care of the rest.

This is the magic formula for manifesting dreams. Now I know that when I completely surrendered everything to God, the Universe took over all the details to make it happen. The same *Intelligence* that transforms the acorn to a mighty oak was quietly working in my favor and I didn't even know it. It's like eating a juicy red watermelon on a hot summer day and spitting the seeds in the ground. You kind of forget about it until you go back to that same spot and see little baby watermelon plants all around.

A little over a year later, I was waiting on tables at the Velvet Turtle Restaurant. I had just gotten home after the lunch shift. By this time, I had written off the music business as just another phase in my life. I figured that things like hit songs happened to "other people," but they weren't meant for me. The phone rang and it was Kevin McGowan, who worked for Al Gallico.

"Al wants to speak to you." "Sure," I said. It had been several months since we had last spoken. "Hello Dahling!" Al said in his thick New York accent. "Shelly West recorded your song!" Shelly West and David Frizzell just had a hit a few months before singing *You're the Reason God Made Oklahoma*. "Oh," I said. "Did you hear me?? Shelly West recorded *Jose*

Cuervo!" I didn't even know I was supposed to be happy about it.

About a week went by and Al called me again. "They want to cut *Jose Cuervo* from the album but I'm fighting for it. Before we're through it's going to be the first single from the album. You wait and see!" "OK," I sighed. If anyone could do it, Al Gallico could. He was a man who made things happen! Still the fact that all of this could be exciting had not quite registered with me yet.

Finally, several days later, Kevin called me and told me to come up to the office. *Jose Cuervo* was going to be Shelly West's next single. Al had an office on Sunset Boulevard in Beverly Hills. I really loved to visit him there. Pat Boone's office was right down the hall.

Once I saw Dick Van Dyke in the elevator. There I was face to face with "Burt" from Mary Poppins. I felt like he was a friend I had never met because for years I had watched his television show. I remember I said, "Hi, I'm Cindy. I already know who you are. Glad to meet you!" He had a warm smile and I instantly liked him.

When I came up to Al's office he played the new recording for me. Al and Kevin were both very happy and excited. I was more confused than ever. For the first time I was hearing someone else singing my song and it sounded so different!

There was a Country Music Club in Marina Del Rey that sometimes invited me to act as a guest DJ. They asked me to come for a special "eat the worm" night and I brought the new recording for all to hear. We were all having a great time and the moment had come to debut the new recording.

I announced the new record and put it on. "Hey everybody, Shelly West recorded *Jose Cuervo* and it's going to be her next single. Within a few lines of the song there was a very negative noise humming from the crowd that began to grow louder and louder. Hundreds of people were booing my poor little song. "Put yours on!" People started yelling so loudly, I ended up stopping the record.

All the way home I sobbed and cried. "It's not fair!" I screamed! Of course Shelley West did a great job of singing and the record was produced extremely well. The crowd was just familiar with mine and the new version seemed strange. It was like hearing someone besides the Beatles sing *I Wanna Hold Your Hand.*

Now I will tell you about that ingenious plan that was in the works while I was busy waiting on tables. All of these facts came to me in bits and pieces after *Jose Cuervo* became 1983 song of the year.

As I told you before, Snuff Garret was one of the judges at the KLAC talent contest that I lost. Did I mention that I was in the first group of elimination? Snuff had produced the music in several Clint Eastwood films and was co-producing Shelly's album with Steve Dorff. Steve told me later that he was not at all interested in recording *Jose Cuervo* with Shelly. He thought it was a novelty song and would never fly.

God is very awesome. I now know that there is no such thing as a coincidence. There are only strategic moves made by the vast intelligence that is running the show. Sitting there on Shelly's session was John Hobbs, the same piano player who played on my session. This was my miracle.

As the producers were having their discussion, John walked over to the conversation and said, "I know this song. I played on Cindy's record." Being the genius he is, within fifteen minutes a chart was written for all the musicians and within half an hour a music track had been laid down. Do I believe in miracles? You bet I do!

Jose Cuervo by Shelly West was released in January of 1983 almost two years after my little record had first been heard on Larry Scott's show. The first time the new version of *Jose Cuervo* appeared on the music charts it came in at #73. Usually in the music industry this means that the song *might* have a slight chance to get in the Top 40. My "Oh, well…" attitude was coming back and my glimmer of hope was dwindling fast.

The first week *Jose Cuervo* jumped to #53. A twenty spot jump in just one week! The second week we were at #43 and things were starting to look good. It made its way up a little more every week until finally, in May of 1983, the week of my twenty-ninth birthday, this surfer girl had written the Number One Country Song in the nation! Yes, *Jose Cuervo* by Shelly West had become a big hit and was surely "a friend of mine!"

I met Shelly West and her mother, Dottie, at the ACM Awards that same week that *Jose Cuervo* was number one. They both looked beautiful with their white dresses and fiery red hair. We were all backstage and when I introduced myself, Shelly gave me a big hug and very happily said, "Thank you for writing that song!" I quickly said, "Thank you for making it a hit!" It was a moment I shall never forget.

Jose Cuervo went on to be the 1983 Country Song of the Year in Billboard Magazine. The next year it was on the list of Grammy nominations. However, it was disqualified because I had recorded it before Shelly came out with her version. They had a rule that year that remakes could not receive a Grammy. Even though my version was known only in Los Angeles, it still went against the rule. I'd like to think I would have won the Grammy. I guess we'll never know. Even today, twenty years later, people refer to *Jose Cuervo* as a classic. I've even heard it referred to as the "National Drinking Anthem of all times"!

I still get excited when I hear it played on the radio or in a club. I'll never forget the first time I ever walked into Pat O'Brien's in New Orleans the summer of 1984. As if on cue the girls at the twin pianos started playing and singing *Jose Cuervo you are a friend of mine!* I was with my brother Mark and it seemed almost planned the way that it happened. Again, there are no coincidences, only amazing gifts from God to remind us that we are on the *Yellow Brick Road*.

Now you know the answer to the question, "How do you make a song a hit?" As I look back I realize that the best part of the whole experience was the journey itself. Experience is a wonderful teacher.

Just recently I was talking with a young friend of mine who had just finished a recording session. Dan was ecstatic as he shared his excitement and pride in the project. I remembered I had the same feeling that day I recorded my version of *Jose*

Cuervo and the first time I ever heard it played on the radio. I looked at him and said very slowly so he would understand, "This is the *it* that you are looking for. It never gets better than this! Savor the moment and embrace the emotion."

As a result of writing *Jose Cuervo* I have met some wonderful people and have made some great lifetime friends. These are my greatest treasures.

I performed at a show in Hollywood where I met Pat Buttram. For a while he invited me as his companion to Hollywood parties where I met a lot of celebrities. Pat is well known for his character, Mr. Haney, in the TV show "Green Acres" and was Gene Autry's sidekick for many years. As we would walk around these functions I'd say, "Pat…I believe these folks think we're doin' something we ain't doin'!" His response was, "I certainly hope so, Cindy Lou!"

One evening we were at a party full of celebrities. There was a band of at least 20 musicians performing and they were playing big band music. Pat asked me if I wanted to sing. He wouldn't take "No" for an answer and after he had a few words with the bandleader I found myself up on stage in front of hundreds of people, many whom I recognized from film and TV.

I felt intimidated, but, I was too nervous to be scared. I instantly thought of my grandmother, Moe. "What the heck," I said to myself and after conferring with the bandleader I belted out *Bill Bailey, Shanty Town* and *Jambalaya*. I decided not to worry about it and just have a good time. That's what Moe would do!

I have a "three song rule". After three songs, I was off the stage and the crowd was applauding wildly. Pat looked at me with pride in his face and told me something I'll never forget. He leaned over and said, "You know why they loved you, Cindy Lou? "Cause you didn't give a *shit* what they thought!" He was a very wise man.

Pat took me to the Brown Derby where he hooked me up with the syndicated columnist Jim Bacon. Jim had been writing about Hollywood for years and knew every star that ever was. Jim and I became great friends and I loved his incredible stories of famous people like Marilyn Monroe, Gary Cooper and Liz Taylor. He was great fun!

One time, we went to lunch and somehow ended up at the Playboy Mansion at George Burns' birthday party. Jim would catch my show at the Palomino Club in North Hollywood and write about me in his column. He always liked my song and I learned a lot from him.

Life would be easier if we all had crystal balls that could tell us the future. I had no idea what the future had in store and if anyone were to tell me, I wouldn't have believed it. I was chasing elusive butterflies and skipping down my *Yellow Brick Road*.

The success of my song should have made me the happiest girl in the world. However, I was spiritually in a very dark place and even though I should have been celebrating life, I was miserable.

About a year after writing Jose Cuervo I had gotten into a romantic relationship that was an emotional roller coaster. When it was good it was the best I had ever known and when it was bad it was the most horrible. Jealousy and insecurity can be extremely toxic and the situation was about to get worse with the success of my song.

Fear is dark and ugly. However, some of the best *Butterfly Moments* are found in what can seem like the darkest moments in your life.

Forgiveness

*"Though I walk through the valley of the shadow of death,
I will fear no evil for thou art with me"*
—Psalm 23

There is fine line at the threshold between life and death. A close call in an accident, an illness or near death experience can bring us face to face with the *other side*. All of these experiences heighten our awareness of the loving presence that is always with us.

My daughter, Denise, convinced me to tell this story in the hopes of helping someone else. It is a painful memory and there are innocents involved. For this reason, I will call this man "Stan".

I met Stan while working as a waitress at Ichabod Crane's. He was good looking, lots of fun and had a wonderful laugh. We fell in love and I would get butterflies every time he'd come in.

Stan took me to pro-football games, nice dinners and walks on the beach. He was eleven years older than I and knew how to treat a lady. He had a wonderful personality and my family loved him. Stan moved in with me and we were very happy.

War is horrible. Severe injuries can be emotional as well as physical. Stan had been in Vietnam and had received three purple hearts. He had been in helicopters that were shot down several times.

Things would be going just great between us and then we'd have an *event*. There was never a witness because they always happened when we were alone. This wonderful man I loved would turn into Mr. Hyde. The ugly ghosts and demons would take over his being and he would turn into a monster.

Stan would insult me, call me names and break things that had sentimental meaning to me. It was always over something trivial. Stan would physically hurt me as well. Once he got angry because I put a navy blue sock with a black one. He threw me on the bed and choked me until I couldn't breathe. The more I fought the more he choked. When I finally went limp he stopped.

Another time he lost it after we had been out with friends. I can't remember exactly what set him off, but he took his Purple Hearts off the wall and broke the glass and the frame his mother had made for him. That night I ended up with a broken rib.

Stan was totally unpredictable and I never knew when these violent acts would occur. Afterwards Stan would cry and cry. With sobs and tears, he would tell me that he loved me and he didn't know why he hurt me. I would feel sorry for him and always take him back. I was pathetically naïve and believed him when he said, "I'll never do it again". The empty promises usually came with flowers or some other kind of gift. Our passions ran deep and I was caught up in a sick drama. It was either heaven or hell and there was no in between.

I have no doubt in my mind that there are beautiful angels and spiritual guides that look out for us. They come to our rescue and sometimes they might even whisper in our ear when we have no idea what to do or where to turn.

It was a beautiful Saturday afternoon in Southern California. Julie was spending the day at my mother's and I had just cleaned the house. I had taken a shower and was sitting in my tiny bathroom painting my toenails.

At first I just felt his presence at the doorway I instinctively could sense that the situation was not good. Nothing had been said, just a bad feeling.

I looked up and saw a loaded .357-magnum pistol pointed at my face. I froze. Stan's blue eyes were dark and threatening and he was speaking in a very low and gravelly voice that I didn't recognize at all. It was as if he was possessed by some kind of demon. "I'm going to kill you and then kill myself," he grumbled in that horrible voice. "No one else will ever have you."

All I could think of was my little girl, Julie. I thought of how her life would be if this happened. I thought about parts of my head decorating the tiny bathroom and the horrible scene that was potentially at hand.

"Did you hear me? I'm going to kill you and then kill myself." That shiny silver gun was now waving around but still pointed at my head. He cocked the trigger.

I was past fear. I knew that if I showed fear I was as good as dead and Julie would have no more *Mommy*. There was nowhere to run. He was blocking the door and I was trapped. The slightest move and I was a goner. The whites of his eyes were yellow and his eyes seemed to be rolling around in chaotic confusion. It was the confusion that would work in my favor.

All of a sudden I heard myself saying, "I'm hungry. Let's go get some Mexican food." Where did that come from?? It was like another person speaking for me while the part that was petrified simply watched.

"I'm going to blow your brains all over this bathroom and then shoot myself." Stan was looking more confused than hateful and I felt in control. A peace came over me and I felt my fear begin to go away. Call it an angel, divine intelligence or a spiritual guide, something or someone had given me the lead and I was following it.

"I feel like some spinach enchiladas. Are you hungry?" Stan was more confused than ever. He kept saying he was going to kill me and I kept talking about Mexican food. Finally, he let that big shiny .357 down to his side.

I got up like nothing had happened and we went to lunch. Before we left I told Stan that I had forgotten something. He stayed in the Bronco and I went back into the house. I found the gun and hid it where he couldn't find it. The next day I took it to my friend, who was a policeman, and told him to "just get rid of it."

Did I leave Stan after that? No. That's how sick I was. Somehow I thought he needed me and this gave me a false sense of self-worth. When you give someone the power to control your self-esteem you are forever at his mercy. My happiness was dependent on him and that was unfair to both of us. It brought feelings of guilt and tremendous pain.

My family was unaware of what was going on with Stan. I was too embarrassed to tell them and I knew that it would shatter the relationship between them. Stan would always brag, "I never cold-cocked you!" He would say this while clenching his fist. There's no telling what my dad or brothers would have done if he had.

I always blamed the war in Vietnam for Stan's behavior. I felt like he was a victim of the war and his problems were a result of his horrific experience. Then one day I realized that *I* was the victim! I would always feel guilty but I hadn't done anything wrong! I was in love with a troubled soul and it was destroying me. One day it finally occurred to me that not everyone who comes home from a war abuses those whom they claim they love. I've never even heard my Dad raise his voice to my mother and he was in the Korean War.

I stayed with Stan because I kept thinking it would get better but it only got worse. It wasn't until a cowboy named Dennis finally came along and took me off on his white horse that I would finally be free from the abuse. The cowboy had seen a friend of his cross that very fragile line of life and death and was afraid it would happen to me.

After getting a desperate phone call from a friend one evening, Dennis had driven to her home but arrived at the tragic scene too late. The woman who had called him was dead, along with her mother. They both had fatal gunshot wounds in their chests. Her husband, who had shot them, was sitting outside on the porch wearing a set of handcuffs and shaking his head. He wasn't even aware of what he had done. The man was in complete denial that he had shot and killed his wife and mother-in-law with his hunting rifle.

Dennis was afraid for me. Looking back I was literally sitting on a time bomb. Dennis probably saved my life when he told me, "Tigers don't change their stripes." This was the magic phrase that finally made me get out of my volatile situation. I always thought it would get better. After all, I kept telling myself, "it was so good at the beginning" and "deep down I know he loves me".

A fearful mind is a fragile thing. There are people who live in darkness because of events that have happened in their lives. Unfortunately, their problems are like garbage that spills on all who are around them. We all have the choice to wallow in misery or learn from it and move on.

For a long time I was not aware from what source I got the idea to suggest Mexican food. I *believed* then but *know* now that it was the power of *Love* that saved me that day. An angel whispered in my ear and saved my life.

Although this was difficult to write, now I can share the story with you. There is never justification in abusing others. No matter what the reason is, when we violate another human being with words or actions or both, we are in essence violating ourselves.

If you have ever been mistreated the *only* cure is forgiveness. This is what Jesus did when he was hanging on the cross. "Father, *forgive* them for they know not what they do!" Forgiveness is an act of love and *Love* is the greatest power in the universe. I have forgiven Stan. The effects from that relationship still show up once in a while but the resentment and anger have all been healed.

I wrote *Jose Cuervo* a few months before I met Stan. I had turned adversity into a motivating force. I guess I wanted to prove something to myself and I never gave up on the dream. *Jose Cuervo* was a great success but my self-esteem was lower than mud on the bottom of a boot. I should have been happy but I was miserable. Now I know that happiness is an inside job and no success on the outside can fix it. This is the false illusion of the ego.

I had a little girl that needed her Mommy. Still filled with mixed emotions and guilt, I finally left Stan, and little Julie and I moved off to greener pastures with the cowboy. This is where my story sounds a lot like a fairy tale. My *Yellow Brick Road* was about to take me to the great state of Texas or, as the cowboys call it, "God's Country!"

Miss Cindy

Cowboys, Cuervo and Texas

*"The stars at night are big and bright
Deep in the heart of Texas."*
—June Hershey

Think of how boring life would be if you ate the same meal, read the same book or stayed in the same room every single day. Of course, if you didn't know any different, I guess it wouldn't matter. In fact, some people are content doing the same routine over and over again. Then there are those of us with passionate souls who are here to learn and experience all that we can. Change is a great teacher. It is through change that we learn and grow.

It was June of 1983, just about one month after *Jose Cuervo* had made the number one spot in the music trades. I had gone to Al Gallico's office to celebrate our success. I brought Al a bottle of Jose Cuervo and took his picture with it. We had come a long way and I felt like part of the gang.

Kevin, Al's assistant, and I had become good friends. He always gave me a lot of encouragement and good advice. In the course of conversation, I learned that there was going to be a music showcase that evening for Craig Dillingham, a new MCA recording artist. Kevin invited me to go. I thought I was just going to a music industry function. Little did I know that I would meet a cowboy who would radically change my life.

I vaguely remember meeting Dennis that evening. Dennis was Craig's business manager. When I first saw him he was standing with his brother, Darryl, in a back room where the artists and musicians all hang out. He was wearing a white suit and a big friendly smile.

The one thing I *do* remember about meeting Dennis was his piercing blue eyes. They had an intriguing look of curiosity. The thing he remembered about me was my handshake. Daddy always taught me that a strong handshake was important but I never dreamed that it would actually win me a husband.

This is how Dennis tells the story of the night we met: On the drive back to their hotel he asked his brother Darryl, "Did you meet that girl who wrote *Jose Cuervo*?"

"I did," Darryl replied.

"Did you shake her hand?? She either knows something I'm supposed to know or she has something that belongs to me."

That night at the Sheraton Universal, Dennis wrote a song about our first encounter. These are the lyrics:

FELL IN LOVE IN A HEARTBEAT
—Dennis Buckingham

I was sittin' in LA feeling down
Me and Wild Turkey goin' round and round
Then I gotta strange feelin'
Like somethin's gonna happen tonight
Then I gotta cold feelin' down deep in my spine
Like somebody somewhere was readin' my mind
You walked in and I knew that the feelin' was right
(chorus)
I fell in love in a heartbeat
True love in a very short time
I knew it was love when I looked up
And your blue eyes met mine
Nothin' was said you just nodded your head
And you wiggled as you walked by
Fell in love in a heartbeat
Now my heart beats for you all night

Now I'm a fun-lovin' guy most all the time
But I saw you and I was on cloud nine
'Cause you 'bout everything any man could need
When you looked at me with them big blue eyes
You just naturally made me high
I felt like a white knight sittin' on a snow white steed

On the night we met, Dennis said a prayer that one day he would have the opportunity to meet me again. You've got to be careful what you pray for!

Al had an office in Nashville, Tennessee called "eleven eleven," that he shared with his partner, Billy Sherrill. It was a converted stately old home located on Music Row. Billy Sherrill was a well-known songwriter and producer in Nashville whose acts included Tanya Tucker, Tammy Wynette and George Jones. In the rear of the building was a recording studio.

About a month after meeting Dennis in Los Angeles, I was in Nashville at the "eleven eleven" studio listening to a song mix. All of a sudden, the door flew open and who do you think walked in? There, with a great big grin on his face, was a cowboy looking at me as if I should know who he was. He says that when he saw me, he looked up and said, "Thank you, God!" This was the beginning of the end of my life as I knew it in Southern California.

After just a short time, Dennis started talking kind of crazy. He told me that I was going to move with him to Texas and we were going to get married and have babies. I told him to "lose my phone number!" He chased and I ran. Finally, after a twenty-eight major city tour promoting Jose Cuervo Tequila for Heublein, I found myself living in DeBerry, Texas.

Dennis told everyone that he "roped and dragged me to East Texas kicking and screaming". Of course this is a very large exaggeration but it is true that I resisted the change as much as I could. I finally surrendered to his persistence with the attitude that I was embarking on a new adventure.

Considering that I had been married before, I consented to marriage with the following condition: "I will marry you under one condition … you always treat me like a girlfriend. The day you treat me like a wife, I am out of here!!" I wanted to keep the romance going. I found out later that flannel pajamas have the same alluring effect on a cowboy as black lace. Yeehaw!!

At the time, DeBerry had one traffic light that blinked yellow, two gas stations and a post office. I went from the Southern California "beach life" to "pure country" living. I even bought a black iron skillet! My daughter Julie was 12 years old then. It was all new to her as well and at first she was surprised to find that there was no "Seven Eleven" to ride her bike to. It almost seemed as if we had moved to a different country!

As I met my new neighbors in Texas, I found them to be extremely friendly. Many times I was asked if I was a *Yankee* because of my accent. Once a man asked me this and when I told him I was from California he said, "You know how they got them folks in California? They lifted up Maine and all the fruits and nuts rolled into the state of California!" I remember he laughed and laughed. I just smiled. I was different and Texans were different, but I was there and soon I had "y'all" in my vocabulary.

Dennis and I were married in December of 1984 and we are sure that I became pregnant with Denise on our honeymoon. I brought Julie to the marriage and he brought Stacey, Kristi and Jessica. It would soon be yours, mine and ours.

We lived on a 125-acre ranch in East Texas that had all kinds of trees including tall pines and majestic oak. The barn was full of beautiful quarter horses and a little retired birthday pony named Princess. We had a gorgeous stud horse whose full name was Super Skipa Star and we called him "Super." He was a dark bay with a white star on his forehead and he was over 16 hands high.

I had just gotten out of an abusive relationship and my emotions were still on shaky ground. This coupled with the fact that I was pregnant and in a state of culture shock caused me to have my *moments*. I remember one time standing in the middle of a pasture screaming, "I married a hick! What am I doing here? I go to places like this on vacation! I miss the beach! Aaghhhhh!!" I felt like a foreigner in a strange land. At least he was a handsome hick.

Love is a great healer and luckily Dennis was patient with me. I was used to pain and the word "trust" had fallen out of my vocabulary. I was like a betrayed, wounded animal, and I had my defense tactics turned on high. My new life on this beautiful East Texas ranch was all just a bit too peaceful and I didn't know how to act.

Julie went to Elysian Fields High School and her whole class consisted of 38 students. It wasn't too long before she had a thick Texas accent. Julie was a straight "A" student and because the school was so small the teachers there gave her special attention. This gave her a better high school experience than she could have ever had in California.

Life was good. I had gone from chaos to peace and it was taking some getting used to. I was learning that the secret to happiness is not having what you want but wanting what you have. I learned to love Texas. She has a way of holding you in her arms and saying, "Welcome home."

Now that I was completely domesticated, it seemed like a good idea to start going to church. It had been 10 years since I had gone on a regular basis. One Sunday morning we all dressed up and took our four girls to the service at St. Lawrence Brindisi in Waskom, Texas.

That first morning as we were walking into the church, I saw a woman with a beautiful smile, just as pregnant as I, walking towards me. We met belly to belly and Donna became my first friend in Texas. We bonded well because it seemed that we were always having the same pregnancy symptoms. Our daughters were both born the next September just three days apart.

When I walked into the church, I saw a piano, but I was a little surprised when no one played it during the service. After church I volunteered to be the piano player. Everyone was excited and I became the new music director at a little country church in Waskom, Texas. It would be here that I would meet friends that would be like family and last a lifetime.

I used this new opportunity to be creative with my music. Now that I was a new mother, I began writing songs for the little children in the church to sing. I was *trying* to get in touch with God through my songwriting and the songs I wrote seemed to come fairly easily to me. This made me think that maybe I was in God's good graces again because I was doing the "church thing" and working with children. What I didn't understand was that God had never left me. Even when I was shootin' down tequila God was always there. I was just still spiritually asleep.

My life had changed from performing in bars and honkytonks to performing at church. I felt like Whoopie Goldberg in *Sister Act* when she plays a Las Vegas entertainer who goes into hiding as a nun and becomes the choir leader.

I had a new husband, a new family, a new set of friends and a beautiful place to live. It would be while living in Texas that I would learn how to wake up and smell the flowers. I had found heaven on earth and the butterflies were everywhere! I just didn't know it, but then, hindsight is 20/20.

The Voice

"Something deeply hidden had to be behind things."
—Albert Einstein
1879–1955
(The Einstein Letter That Started It All)

Tell a cowboy that you would like to have babies and he will be happy to oblige! I moved to Texas in September of 1984 and a year later Denise Michelle was born. I learned that nursing does *not* prevent pregnancy. Fifteen months later Jordan Taylor was born which between the two of us made five girls and a boy. It was time to shut down the baby factory.

It was during this time of transition and new "mommyhood" that I first became aware of what I now refer to, as *The Voice*. It was very subtle and quiet at first. I found myself filled with new creativity and musical ideas I thought were mine.

I decided to take some of my royalties from *Jose Cuervo* and produce a children's album with the new songs I was writing. The more I worked on my new children's music project the more I realized this was more than just a good idea. I was being led.

Anytime I wanted to write a song, I found that all I had to do was "ask" and then not think about it. All of a sudden while doing dishes or changing a diaper an idea would pop into my head and a new song would be born. Many times the song was finished before I had a chance to write it down. Sometimes I wrote more than one in a day.

It is amazing what beautiful ideas float in when you allow them to. It's like being a window, with the curtains wide open, letting the sun shine into a room. They are magical *Butterfly Moments* of inspiration that seem to come from nowhere.

I had written several songs and now I needed to find the children to sing on the new music project. I put the word out and within a week I had met all of the children I needed for the album. There were only four.

I had heard of a family that sang at a local church. There were two sisters, Lisa and Erin, and they both sang like angels. Their father brought them over to the ranch one evening and they were amazing. Lisa had strawberry blonde hair and a lovely smile. She was 12 at the time and her voice was full and beautiful. Erin was 8 with brown curly hair and her little face was as sweet as her crystal clear voice.

I called Julie's teacher, Alice Langley, and told her I needed a little bitty voice that could sing on key. She brought over her 6-year-old daughter, Lexi and she turned out to be perfect! Lexi had great big eyes and long shiny brown hair. Now I had three singers.

My fourth little singer, Sabrina, had sold me some Girl Scout cookies. I instantly fell in love with her. We stayed in touch through her mother, Jennifer, who happened to be our "mail lady". Nine-year-old Sabrina had a face like those you see in a vintage portrait. She had sandy blonde hair and big green eyes. She brought what would later be referred to as "the sound" to the project. I love her like one of my own.

We recorded the album at Red River Studios about 30 miles away in Bossier City, Louisiana. At the time the owner, Charles Smith, was doing music projects with Richard Wells and Ron Capone. Richard is a musical genius. He played every instrument on every song. This was amazing to watch not just because of his amazing talent but also because Richard Wells is blind.

Ron Capone has amazing ears and created our sound. Ron had been the engineer on some giant recordings, including Otis Redding's *Dock of the Bay*. He also won the Grammy for his work on the soundtrack for the film *Shaft*. It was an honor to work with both of these awesome talents.

There is no doubt that this project was being led with some kind of divine direction. The four children sang every song four times so the four voices became sixteen. Ron was very impressed with their combined sound. Each brought a unique quality and together it was like one beautiful voice that literally brought tears to my eyes.

I remember the evening we listened to *Heavenly Light* after stacking all of the harmonies. The children sang every harmony part individually. I had written the parts and up until that point the outcome was only in my head. When I actually heard the result for the first time, I began to cry soft, warm tears. Little Sabrina was very concerned. She looked up at me with those big green eyes and said, "Miss Cindy, did we do it wrong?"

I was touched. "No baby, you sound like a beautiful choir of angels!" I replied.

I called the music project *Let's Celebrate*. After the first album was finished the children and I formed the Kids for Kids Ministry. The purpose of the Ministry was to teach children self-esteem through helping other, less fortunate, children. We invited children, who in turn invited other children from all different denominations and our choir of 4 grew to a choir of 35.

When we recorded the last ten songs we chose John Hodges, Janna and Jennifer Jennings and my daughter Denise from the choir, to sing with the original four. Denise was only three years old at the time. She did amazingly well and I was incredibly proud of her. Denise sang a solo on the song *I Promise* and performed it perfectly on the second take! The whole project is a timeless treasure.

The children in East Texas are taught good manners. When my children were in the younger grades there was actually a place on their report card that said, "Says yes, ma'am and no, ma'am." The children call adults by their first name, with Mr. or Miss in front of it. I was no longer Cindy Jordan shooting tequila and dancing on tables. I was now "Miss Cindy" with a music ministry for children.

The Kids for Kids Choir sang at fairs and festivals all over the Ark-La-Tex. We visited hospitals and little country churches where we passed a "love basket" for St. Jude's Hospital. A local cable station heard of the ministry and together we produced three television shows called *Let's Celebrate*. The show was kind of like a Christian version of Sesame Street.

At first I thought that *The Voice* was just my imagination, but the more that things fell into place the more I knew it was much more than my imagination at work. I would tell people that I didn't write the songs alone and that all of the music was co-written by God. Part of me thought this sounded *cute*, but the deepest part of me realized that it was true.

The Voice let me know that I was to finish three albums. We sold several thousand on television and some of the stories that came back to us were incredible. I remember one lady wrote and said that she bought a set of tapes for the neighbor child who lived in the apartment next door. The child's parents were alcoholics and, when things got rough, she could hear the little girl through the wall, crying in her room. She said that after she gave the little girl the *Let's Celebrate* tapes instead of crying, she could hear the child playing the tapes.

Before we would perform I would always tell the children and their wonderful parents, "We're making memories!" There is one personal memory that instantly comes to mind.

We were on our monthly visit to the Shriner's Hospital in Shreveport, Louisiana. I was playing the piano and the children were all on stage singing *Jesus Loves the Children*.

My little three-year-old Denise was obviously enjoying being on stage in the front row. This was her opportunity to be *A Star*! She started with the "Elvis lip." This is when half of the top lip goes up and down. She then combined that gesture with the "Elvis knee," a kind of a circular motion. The children all began to giggle. With that, Denise turned around, bent over and shook her little fanny at the audience.

By this time I was flushed with nervous fever and the kids were looking at her, finding it hard to sing. The more she showed her stuff the more giggles were released throughout the choir, as well as from the audience. However, being the pro that I am, I didn't stop playing the music. I have to admit it was funny, but Denise's timing was obviously inappropriate.

 Finally, the grand finale! Denise started to lift her skirt up and down to reveal her lacy little panties. Luckily by then the song was just about over. Her Daddy finally came over and gently removed her from the stage. She was not happy about this and she fussed a little. I have to admit, she was quite the entertainer. While all of the memories with the kids are wonderful, we still have a good laugh over that one.

Sadly enough, as the children grew older our choir got smaller. We tried to recruit more children, but it was never quite like the original group. I remember my friend, Benjamin, once said to me, "Cindy, some people come in your life for a reason and some people come for a season." Childhood seems like the shortest season of all. I heard a great quote that captures this. "The days are long, but the years are short."

I used to confuse *The Voice* with imagination. After all why would God ever want to talk to me? This only happens to people like Noah, Moses and Neale Donald Walsch. It's hard to describe *The Voice* because it is the language of the soul. It's just something that you know.

The Voice is silent and beautiful. It possesses all wisdom and its only emotion is love. *The Voice* has been with us forever and when it speaks, the soul understands because it rings with love and truth.

Many of the original Kids for Kids Choir members are now married with families of their own. I knew back then that, one day, something wonderful would happen with the three *Let's Celebrate* albums, but it just wasn't the right time. Just recently, twelve years later, a record company has decided to run with the project. The songs have been translated into different languages including Spanish and Chinese and the CDs are being sold all over the world. There are a few *Butterfly Moments* worth mentioning before I share, as Paul Harvey would say, "the rest of the story."

Living in East Texas taught me the value of simplicity. It was all part of the perfect plan designed just for me on the journey down my very own *Yellow Brick Road*. In the plan I have connected and intersected with many other *Yellow Brick Roads*. I am honored that I am connecting with you now. At this point I would like to personally thank you for reading my story. I wrote it for *you*, I already know it.

You have a loving presence with you always. If any of my story has made a difference to you then let's have a *Butterfly Moment* now. If not, keep reading. There are some more amazing miracles I want to share!

The Day I Learned How to Pray

*"Who entrusts himself to God
has also placed the world within the Hands
to which he has himself appealed
for comfort and security."*
—A Course in Miracles

It was a regular Saturday afternoon on the ranch. I was doing my normal Saturday "stuff" when the door burst open and Dennis ran in carrying Denise. He laid our little six-year-old baby girl down with her face up to the ceiling. She had on a red hooded sweatshirt and blue jeans. Her long blonde hair was spread out all over the couch and she looked frightened to tears.

Dennis was holding up two fingers. "How many fingers do you see, baby?" "I don't know," she said with her bottom lip quivering. He held up three fingers. "How many now?" I don't know, Daddy, I can't see any-fing."

With that, Dennis swooped her up and out the door they ran. They jumped in the brown Taurus and sped off. In the meantime, I grabbed Jordan and took him to a neighbor's house. My heart was racing and I was scared.

Dennis had been in the barn saddling up a young gray horse for the first time. This was a new experience for the horse and when Dennis put on the bridle, she reared up and fell backwards with her head and upper body in the stall but her lower body in the walkway. He was unaware that little Denise was in the barn.

The horse was frantically thrashing and kicking around with its hooves outside the stall trying to get up. Little Denise loves animals and, as little kids do, she ran over to help the horse. When she did, the horse kicked her square on the side of her head, like a bat hitting a pinata. This sent Denise flying about four feet off the ground across the center of the barn. When she hit the wall, as Dennis describes it, " she slid down just like water."

At first, she wasn't moving, and Dennis thought she was dead. Little

Denise was out cold. He said later that it was "a thousand wonders" that she could survive such a hard blow. Now, my baby couldn't see. This would be the day I would learn how to pray.

As I drove the truck to the hospital, I remember the tall pine trees lined up on both sides of the highway. They looked so powerful and majestic to me. It was as if they had a sense of *knowing* that all was happening exactly the way it was supposed to. Looking back, I realize now my soul knew this. However, inside my human self was the feeling of complete chaos. Now I understand that the stately pine trees were silently whispering, "There is perfect order in the universe."

People in other cars were acting normal. How could they? Didn't they realize that my baby was hurt?? I felt so alone and insignificant. I had never felt so small and helpless. This was way beyond my control and I was totally at the mercy of the universe. There was a deafening silence in the truck and I felt like I was in some kind of bad dream. I started talking to God.

I guess I figured I should pray but I hardly knew where to begin. I started talking out loud and my conversation with God went something like this: "Dear Lord, Please let Denise… God…This sounds ridiculous. I don't even know if I'm saying the "right words". You already know what *I* want. This is so obvious. I am not even going to insult your intelligence by asking you to save my baby".

At this point my stomach sank and my heart felt heavy. All tension had left my body and I felt like I could melt away in a puddle and disappear forever. It was a moment of complete *trust* and *surrender*. I continued.

"OK, God…there are three things that can happen here. Number one: Denise is going to be blind. Number two: we're going to lose her. Number three: she's going to be fine and healthy and be my happy little girl again. Of course, I want number three however, if you decide on one or two I just ask that you give me the strength to deal with the hand I am dealt. I am trusting your decision."

That was it. It was all in God's hands, but, then it always was. I just acknowledged that the outcome would be what it was meant to be and

I completely trusted God. With my profound *surrender* came the most awesome peace I have ever known.

When the doctor saw Denise, he was not very reassuring. As she laid on the table, her eyes were rolling around and she could not see anything. The doctor kept shaking his head with a very grim look on his face.

I could see that Dennis was nervous. He had witnessed the impact of the accident, so this was harder on him. He had no idea that Denise was even near the barn but the accident happened on "his watch" and he was filled with guilt as well as concern. I had prepared myself and was ready to deal with whatever I had to deal with. After a very long eighteen hours in Pediatric ICU, Denise regained her sight and we were able to take her home.

On reflection, I can still feel that sense of wisdom of those pine trees lined up along the highway as I drove to the hospital. They seemed so calm when it seemed my world had just caved in. That's the beautiful thing about Mother Nature. She never gets off course when chaos sets in because she knows there is order in the chaos.

While writing this story and sharing it with my daughter, Denise, she shared her version of the story. She told me she remembers "sneaking" in the barn that day. Denise has only one memory from the moment she was kicked until she woke up and saw us with the doctor at the hospital. Denise says that as her Daddy drove her to the emergency room, she could see herself lying in his lap through the windshield from the hood of the car. Denise had an out of body experience, which I would classify as a very memorable *Butterfly Moment* for her. She says that as she watched her hurt little body she had a complete feeling of peace but she was concerned for her Daddy.

How To Pray

I heard a great story from my friend Phil Brown about an experiment that was done at Harvard University,

There were three small strawberry gardens that were put into three separate rooms. In the first room, the strawberry plants were watered and given plenty of sunlight. Nice, healthy strawberries grew on the plants and they were tasty and sweet.

In the second room, the strawberry plants were watered and given plenty of sunlight. In this room, there was a prayer said every day over the strawberries. "Dear Lord, Please let these strawberries grow as big as plums!" Sure enough, the strawberries grew as big as plums and they were tasty and sweet.

In the third room, the strawberry plants were watered and given plenty of sunlight. In this room, everyday, there were four words said over the strawberries. "Thy will be done." The strawberries grew as big as peaches and they were delicious.

Is there anything God can't do? Why do we think we can do it better? I think we put too many human limitations on God and God's capabilities. Think of a good friend. You have a ten-pound bag of sugar in your pantry. If that friend asked to borrow a cup of sugar would you give him some? Of course you would and your friend would have no doubt that you would gladly give it to him.

Would your friend go to a stranger and ask for a cup of sugar? Would you? Probably not. Why? Because you don't *know* that person. If you don't know him, then you can't trust him. There's no telling what condition that sugar is in or if he will even give you any. It's not likely that you will knock on a stranger's door to ask for a cup of sugar.

If your friend comes to the door and the sugar is full of tiny little bugs, would you give him a cup? NO! Why? Because you love your friend and the sugar is contaminated. Instead, you give your friend a cup of honey, which is actually much healthier than sugar anyway.

If your friend comes to the door and says, "Gee, I know you have plenty of sugar. I hope you'll give me a cup. Maybe you don't like me enough or maybe I don't deserve it. Pleeeeeeze, can I have some sugar? I hope you have enough for me".

Pretty pathetic, huh? I for one would feel badly if a good friend had any doubt that I would not honor such an easy request. I would be happy to give him *anything* that was in my power to give. Name one thing that God *cannot* give!! We need to understand that God will *always* honor the greater good.

How many times when we "borrow" a cup of sugar do we come back with a cup to replace it? If you gave a cup of sugar to a friend, would you be angry if he didn't bring you a cup in return? Of course not! You probably gave it with no condition. It was just a *friendly* thing to do and you were glad to *do it*. Giving with no condition is incredibly empowering!

God's got plenty of sugar!! He has an abundance of sugar! God gives unconditionally. When you *know* God, it is easy to ask for the sugar. When you don't know God, you can't trust God. God won't give us anything that might be bad for us. God loves us with all that is and celebrates when we finally *know* this.

Sometimes people pray and pray and pray. God already knows our prayers. When we ask God for anything, we always get an answer. The problem is, we are not quiet and do not listen!! How can we learn the answer if we just keep asking the question?

Now whenever I have a situation and I have a "doubt thought" I simply say, "You know my deepest desires. I completely trust You and I know You are taking care of the details. Just let me know what I have to do."

Most of the time I just think of the strawberry plants and simply say, "*Thy will be done.*" There is no doubt in my mind that everything that happens in my life is because I am loved and I am discovering that *I am Love*.

When you develop a personal relationship and finally *know* God, there is an awareness that is almost magical. Everyday you can see hundreds of miracles you never noticed before.

Dreams come true and miracles happen. Every day of your life expect a miracle and you will have *Butterfly Moments* that will absolutely blow you away!

The Bookstore

"For nothing happens by accident in God's world, and there is no such thing as a coincidence."
—Neale Donald Walsch
(Conversations With God)

Some of my favorite Butterfly Moments are the ones that some people think of as coincidence. The word "coincidence" comes from the word "coincide" which means to take up the same place in space.

There are those who might say that a coincidence is purely accidental, or something that happens "just by chance," like a roll of the dice. When you understand that there is a perfectly designed plan, custom-made just for you in your life's journey, the events referred to as "coincidence" can be some of the best and most memorable *Butterfly Moments* in your life.

I made some wonderful friendships in Texas that will last throughout my lifetime. Living in the country, I learned a sense of community that I had never known before. The people I knew in East Texas were friendly and always seemed to be there to help each other out. Once, I ran out of gas because my gas gauge was not working. I was stranded by the side of the road. This happened on a farm road where there was very little traffic. I got help right away and during the twenty minutes I stood at the side of the road, at least a dozen people stopped to see what they could do.

I moved to East Texas in October of 1984 and by December of 1986 I had two little babies. My life had changed dramatically and I loved the fact that I was a new mother again. I was working with the *Kids for Kids Choir* and we performed about once a month at various fairs, festivals and small country churches all over the Ark-La-Tex.

The choir had finished three albums. We sold the *Let's Celebrate* tapes at our shows to raise money for different children's charities. Because the songs were original, the group had their own unique identity. The children were precious and gave so much of themselves. We had made up hand routines to the choruses of the songs using signing. They sang with their voices and their hands. Watching them perform was enchanting.

The music industry can be very brutal, as I had learned. This kept me from exposing the *Let's Celebrate* music to anyone in the music business. I was afraid of any kind of negative criticism. I guess I thought any negative feedback would shatter my belief that God had inspired the songs I wrote. I had written and produced the albums and the children sang like little angels. My Dad designed the covers and the whole music project was very close to my heart. I had been very protective, but at the same time I wanted to share the music with the world outside of my own.

Fear can freeze you in your tracks and I had a really bad case of *fear of rejection*. After weeks and weeks of pondering, I decided to take the *Let's Celebrate* project to a big Christian bookstore in Shreveport, Louisiana. I finally mustered up the courage to go. I was a nervous wreck! There were all kinds of funny feelings in my stomach and I felt hot with emotional fever.

I recruited my friend, Donna, to come with me for moral support. We drove my big white "mommy" station wagon. On the ride to Shreveport I remember looking at Donna and saying, "You know we're not alone. The backseat is full of angels and they are all on our side." There was a part of me that was hoping this was true but, looking back, there was also a part of me that *absolutely knew* it was true. Later, I would find out that angels were definitely with us.

When we arrived at the bookstore, all kinds of thoughts were racing through my head and I was sharing them out loud with Donna. "What if they don't like it? I will be crushed!" Fear and doubt had completely taken over. "Wonder if all of this *assignment from God stuff* was just my imagination??" I felt that if I were turned away, my faith would be destroyed. This was the scariest thought of all. Donna was assuring me that everything was going to turn out great, but I could see her concern.

We talked for several minutes before we finally got out of the car. Then very slowly and cautiously, we walked across the parking lot and into the bookstore. We asked to see the person in charge. As we waited for her, I walked around looking at the different displays. The store had a pleasant atmosphere and I was happy that I had finally found the courage to come.

After about twenty minutes, a very tall woman appeared and my nervous feelings quickly returned. She was wearing a slate gray dress, orthopedic shoes and her hair was piled high into a beehive bun, all of which made her about 6 feet tall. The no-nonsense look on her face reminded me of the head matron of a woman's prison.

When I get excited and nervous I start talking. A lot! As soon as I opened my mouth, no matter how much I tried, there was no way I could turn it off. I was talking a mile a minute, digging my hole deeper and deeper as I spoke. I guess I thought as long as I kept talking the woman couldn't say "No". Donna was staring at me with big expressive eyes that were screaming, "For the love of God… STOP TALKING!"

Finally my sweet friend lightly touched my arm and said quietly, "Cindy, why don't you play the music so she can hear it." I abruptly stopped. Somehow, Donna was able to find my mute button. The lady looked a bit relieved and agreed to listen. Anything to shut me up.

The woman led us into another room that had about a dozen cubicles for listening to music. We walked over to a tape machine and she put in one of the tapes. I felt like I was in some kind of dream state as we listened to the children singing *Jesus Loves the Children*. I had no sense of reality and my legs felt like spaghetti noodles.

All of a sudden from behind one of the cubicles we could hear someone shouting with incredible excitement, "That's Cindy Jordan! That's Cindy Jordan!"

What in the world? Was I hearing things?

The lady who belonged to the voice was still sitting in a cubicle and we could only hear her as she called out again, "That's Cindy Jordan! I know her!" As we turned towards where the voice was coming from, up popped a very attractive woman with sandy blonde hair that was pulled back into a ponytail.

She came over to where the three of us were standing. Still full of excitement she exclaimed, "That's Cindy Jordan! That's Cindy Jordan! I know her! I know her!"

My emotions switched from fear to confusion, but they were still intense. "I'm Cindy Jordan," I said with a baffled look on my face. "Cindy!" she screamed with excitement. "Remember me from the Polk Salad Festival? You brought your *Kids for Kids Choir* to sing."

Even while under this feeling of intense emotion and despite all that was happening, my memory of the festival was vaguely coming back. I had brought the *Kids for Kids* choir to sing and the children had performed on a flat bed trailer. I stood there speechless, which is unusual for me. All I could do was nod my head.

She went on. "You gave me one of the *Let's Celebrate* tapes. It saved my grandson's life!" By now, I was a basket case and it felt as if an emotional elevator was going up and down out of control between my heart and my throat. My friend Donna and the very tall woman looked on, just as baffled and surprised as I was.

"Last Halloween, some friends from church organized a hayride. My grandson was sitting towards the back of the trailer. We hit a bump and he fell out, hitting his head on the road. It was a hard blow and he wouldn't come to. The doctors were not sure of his prognosis. They said there was even a chance he would never wake up again. I went to Wal-Mart and bought an auto-reverse tape machine so that it could play both sides of your tape non-stop. He loved that tape so much and I instructed the nurses to never let the music stop playing. I wanted him to know that he was never alone and that Jesus loved him. Your songs brought him back to life!" She went on to tell me that he had been in a coma for two weeks before finally waking up.

I can hardly describe the emotional feeling that came over me. All I could do was stare at her in awe as the tears fell freely down my cheeks. I was shaking everywhere and it felt like my knees were going to give out.

I had even forgotten the reason why we had come to the bookstore. All I could think of was that sweet little boy falling off the hay truck, lying there in a hospital listening to songs like *Jesus Is My Best Friend* and *I Believe In Love*. It was a beautiful *Butterfly Moment* that even now seems to be permanently suspended in time.

Some might call this event a "coincidence". I know that the fact that this wonderful woman was in *that* bookstore at *that* particular moment in time was all part of an exquisitely orchestrated plan. After this beautiful encounter, my question "Is this my imagination or am I really being guided?" never again crossed my mind. This was by far the greatest reward I could have ever hoped for.

Donna was in complete awe and the very tall woman had a beautiful warm smile on her face. The woman told me that she would be happy to not only sell my tapes, but that she would show me how to effectively sell my tapes to other retailers. I went from being afraid of her to seeing that she was a warm, friendly, and loving woman. I realized that my fear was just a bad illusion I had created in my mind.

As we were driving home Donna started humming the theme song to the old television show, *The Twilight Zone*. She was the one who first brought to my attention that this was an extra-ordinary experience. I was still in the afterglow of an amazing *Butterfly Moment*. All I could think about was a little boy in the hospital listening to the children singing songs that had been inspired to me. For this, I felt deeply honored.

I found out later that his grandmother had dropped by the bookstore because she had a little time between appointments. It had never been her intention to even be there that day.

There is no such thing as coincidence. When you realize this you look at events in your life and the people you meet in a completely different way. It might be someone standing next to you in a checkout line or someone you meet in a waiting room. Anyone at anytime can make a difference in your life and you can make a difference in theirs as well.

When I desperately needed an angel, this beautiful woman appeared from nowhere. It was a beautiful *Butterfly Moment* I hold dear in my heart. We are all here to learn from each other. When the lesson is *love* you can be sure that it is God's perfect plan working in harmony with the universe.

The Airplane Ride

"We must laugh and we must sing,
We are blest by everything
Everything we look upon is blest."
—William Butler Yeats
1865-1939
(Dialogue of Self and Soul)

Have you ever sat next to someone on an airplane who tells you something that has an unforgettable impact on your life? There is something about the conversations we have in the air. I have had people tell me things that they say they normally don't tell anyone, let alone a stranger. Then after sharing an amazing story, we barely speak at the baggage claim. Even after exchanging phone numbers, very rarely have I ever reconnected. It's an interesting phenomenon.

The greatest rewards I have received as a result of writing music are those special times that I learned first hand that I had touched somebody's life. Money is nice but I have learned that money is only *part* of the love energy that we draw to ourselves. When we are on purpose and in harmony with the loving universe, we are compensated generously every day.

If you only look for payback in the illusory form of money you miss out on the thousands of other blessings that are present in every moment. It only takes a slight shift in your awareness to realize these many rewards. It's all about looking at life and its treasures through your spiritual eyes.

I remember the first time I heard *Jose Cuervo* on the radio. I was so excited! People I had never met were actually listening to my song. Then I took it a step further and realized that eventually people might even sing my song. Maybe they'd sing it at parties, or while doing every day things like washing the car or taking a shower. We all sound so good when we sing in the shower. Little did I know that one day I would actually catch someone in the act!

I was on an airplane with my children. We were on our way to Shreveport from Atlanta and had stopped in Monroe, Louisiana. As we were waiting for people to board the plane I heard a man behind me singing, "Jose Cuervo you are a friend of mine."

I smiled to myself. It had to be someone I knew or someone who had seen me sing before. The man did it again. In a kind of mumbled tone I heard him sing those familiar lyrics I had written years before. "Jose Cuervo you are a friend of mine."

At this point I turned around. "Hello," I said. The man looked up and said hello. He was polite but not friendly. It was obvious he had things on his mind. He was shuffling around a lot of papers in his briefcase. He would pick them up and read each one briefly just as you would when going over your notes before a big presentation. Then I heard the man sang it again! "Jose Cuervo you are a friend of mine."

I turned around again, smiled and said, "Hello". He seemed a bit annoyed. The man had on reading glasses and was looking at me over the top of them. He acted as if I was interfering with his concentration. "Hello," he grunted. I turned back around a little confused.

After a minute or two he sang it again! *Jose Cuervo you are a friend of mine.* Again I smiled and looked over the back of my seat. "OK," I said. "Who are you?" Because so many people from Shreveport knew me from this song I was sure he was teasing me and playing some kind of a game. After all, what are the chances that someone would be singing my song out of the clear blue??

"Excuse me?" he replied.

"Who are you?" I asked again. It was clear he was not interested in friendly conversation. The man told me his name. Again he was polite, but even less friendly. I turned back around. He sang it again! *Jose Cuervo you are a friend of mine.*

"OK," I said with a "c'mon, quit pulling my leg" kind of tone. "How do I know you?" I had a big grin on my face. His look of annoyance was as clearly defined as my smile.

"I don't believe I know you," he said with a *please leave me alone* tone in his voice.

"You don't *know* me??" I started becoming incredibly excited. "You mean you don't know me and you were just singing that song off the top of your head??"

"What song?" he said looking a bit dazed and confused.

"You were just singing *Jose Cuervo you are a friend of mine*. You mean you don't even know you were singing it??"

I was getting more and more excited by the second. "You were singing it with your subconscious?" My voice dramatically amplified.

Still looking a bit baffled he slightly shook his head and said, "I suppose I was."

"O My God!! O My God!! This is great!!" Isn't it funny how we say "God" when really cool things happen. I was so excited by now that I was actually making a scene. "You are telling me that you don't know me and you were just singing *Jose Cuervo you are a friend of mine* off the top of your head?? I WROTE THAT SONG!! I always knew that people I had never met would be singing it in their everyday lives but I never caught anyone actually doing it!!"

I was so caught up in the moment that I was not aware that other people on the plane had been watching this exchange and were clearly amused. The whole event was way cool! It felt as if I had hit some kind of jackpot and bells and whistles were going off everywhere.

The seating space in an airplane is pretty small and the passengers who were sitting close by were all laughing. By this time, even the man who had been singing my song was laughing. We both shared a magical moment that we will never forget. Just think, you are casually singing a song while going over some business notes and totally unbeknownst to you the songwriter of that song is sitting in an airplane seat in front of you.

As news of the event that was taking place traveled to the other passengers, cards and napkins started showing up on my tray table. I must have signed 25 airplane napkins. It was obvious that there were a lot of country music fans on the plane that day.

Denise and Jordan were just little toddlers at the time. They were even giggling as they watched their Mommy get excited and carry on. I'll never forget that wonderful man, with his briefcase, looking over the top of his glasses at me with that bewildered look on his face.

Some people might say this was just a coincidence. I can't help but feel sorry for them. I know deep in my heart that this event was a gift from the universe. It was a lovely affirmation that whenever we are on purpose, we touch the lives of others. Just think of all that had to happen to put *that* businessman and me together on *that* airplane at *that* same moment in time. I think of all that had to happen for him to even know the song. It was a *Butterfly Moment* I will never forget. I wish I knew his name. I guess it really doesn't matter.

From The Other Side

"A sonnet is a moment's monument-
Memorial from the soul's eternity
To one dead deathless hour"
Dante Gabriel Rosetti
1828–1882
(Sonnets from the House of Life)
— Betty Jane Grigg
1971–1989

It was Sunday night, October 1, 1989. I had just put a load of laundry away and happened to look at the clock on the VCR. It was 10:23 p.m. and I vaguely remember seeing some sort of car accident was on the news. All of a sudden I heard a horrible scream come from Julie's bedroom.

I ran into Julie's room and her eyes were half closed. "What's wrong, Baby?" I could see that she was not hurt but it was clear that she was frightened about something. All of a sudden she started saying, "I love God, I love God, I love God" over and over again. She was frantic.

"Julie!" my voice was loud and firm.

"Oh, Mommy! Just hold me. I love God, I love God!" she whimpered. I sat with her and stroked her hair until she finally went back to sleep. By this time Dennis had come into the room.

"What's wrong with Julie?" He said with concern.

"I guess she had a nightmare," I said, completely puzzled. I had never seen her do anything like this before.

The next morning at 6:45 we got a phone call. It was Denise and Jordan's babysitter, Sandra Goswick. I could hear by her tone that this was not good. "Did you hear about BJ Grigg," she asked.

"No," I answered.

"She was killed in an accident last night." BJ had been involved in that head on collision that I'd seen on television the night before. BJ was Julie's best friend.

BJ was on her way to a church function when a car from the opposite side of the interstate lost control, crossed the easement and hit her car head-on. BJ was a gorgeous girl and even more beautiful on the inside. She loved working with small children and was a pure joy to be around. The news hit hard and deep. The Griggs were our close friends. They are a beautiful family and when the girls became best friends they welcomed us to all of their family functions. Lou Ann, BJ's mother, used to have pizza parties for the kids all the time and her home was a gathering spot for teenagers. BJ's brother, Gurvais, was like a big brother to Julie. BJ's daddy, Clayton, treated Julie like his own.

I went into Julie's room. She had just gotten ready for school. When I told her the news she gasped and her eyes got very big. "It was BJ! It was BJ!" trying to catch her breath. "Mommy, it was BJ!" she cried. "I was lying in bed and my legs and my arms started going up in the air. It was like someone was trying to take me out of my body! It felt so weird, Mommy! I thought I was dying!"

When I heard Julie scream the VCR said 10:23 p.m. I found out later that BJ was declared dead at 10:25 p.m. "BJ loves you so much Julie and the two of you have shared everything. Death is a beautiful experience and BJ was sharing it with you."

Losing a young, close friend of the family was a pain like I had never known. There is a distinct cry like no other when a woman loses her baby. It is the saddest, most penetrating, sound in the universe. I can still hear Lou Ann's wailing cry as she grabbed Julie and hugged her at the funeral home. "Oh Julie, BJ loved you so much!"

We found out later that BJ had been counseling some girls at a church function and said something to the girls that they thought strange at the time. "I am going to die very soon," she told them with tears running down her cheeks. "I don't mind because I know I will be with my Father in heaven. I am just so sad for my family because I know it will hurt them." She said things like this to Julie as well. Somehow, BJ knew.

On October 19, eighteen days after BJ's accident we were at the breakfast table. It was Julie's seventeenth birthday. She casually said, "BJ came to see me again last night to wish me Happy Birthday. This time I knew it was her, so I wasn't scared. Bye, Mom." She drank down her orange juice and was out the door to go to school. I sat there stunned. At the same time I thought of how wonderful it was to understand that your best friend was not gone, just on the *other side*.

LYNE PACE
1976–1992

Young people have so much energy and passion for life and no one had more than Lyne Pace. I'll never forget the day her father, Roy, first brought her to the ranch. Roy was working with Dennis and commuting from Elkart, Texas. Lyne was wearing pink. She had on a big pink bow, pink shorts, pink socks and a pink shirt. Lyne had the most beautiful smile on a ten-year-old I have ever seen. Her laughter was contagious, and I fell in love with her on the spot.

We had Dennis's girls, Stacey, Kristi and Jessica, every summer and Lyne became part of our family. For three years she spent every summer with us and would stay for weeks at a time. Lyne was a gorgeous girl with long, blonde hair and an impish way that made her quite a character to be around. I remember one time Dennis had given her $20 for helping me clean the house. She was always eager to please and she loved money! She asked for her payment in ones and for days Lyne walked around the house smelling the 20 new bills, fanning herself with the green money.

We got that horrible call June 8, 1992. I couldn't believe it!! A deep feeling of pain and loss went all through me as I heard Roy say, "We lost Lyne."

"Oh no!" I screamed. "We're on our way."

Lyne had gone with a friend to MacDonald's to get french-fries. She loved MacDonald's french-fries! On the way home, Lyne was thrown from a truck when her friend lost control just a few blocks from her house. Her friend survived.

When we arrived, Tara, Lyne's sister, was in the front yard. She told us that her baby sister had been thrown out of a truck. Inside were Roy and Johnny, Lyne's mother. She was crying with that same keening sound I had heard from BJ's mother, Lou Ann, a few years before. If you've ever heard it once, you know it again.

When we went to the funeral home during the next days, it seemed so unreal. Lyne was a donor and the little shell I saw in the coffin was not our sweet baby. It was just the remaining evidence that Lyne had been with us for a short time in our physical world. Now she would be with us spiritually. Oh, yes! Lyne hadn't gone anywhere quite yet.

It started off with weird little things at first. Lyne's sister, Tara and I began comparing notes.

I put the music together for her funeral and when I tried to play the music strange things were happening with the tape. At first it played really fast and it sounded like the chipmunks singing. Then it completely rewound on its own. Tara and I looked at each other and somehow we knew it was Lyne.

At Lyne's house, Max, their German shepherd would look up at the ceiling while running in circles barking. One afternoon while I was talking to Tara on the phone, she saw Lyne's ethereal form glide across their hallway. Tara gasped and then after a long pause she quietly said, "I just saw Lyne." She said that Lyne was shimmering and looked beautiful.

At our house I would take off my earrings at night and lay them together on my dresser. Several times when I woke up the next morning I would find one earring on the dresser and one on the windowsill in the bathroom.

All kinds of weird little things would happen that we thought were our imagination, and probably just wishful thinking that Lyne was still with us. Things would move and doors would open on their own. I remember a glass flying across the dining room one day and thinking that Lyne must be frustrated.

Going to her grave was always surreal. I'll never forget going back to the car with the children and seeing my 5-year-old son Jordan still sitting at Lyne's grave. He was holding a ball and seemed to be in a trance. I walked back over to him. "C'mon baby," I said. He looked up at me with big solemn eyes.

Quietly he said, "I was talking to Lyne, Mama."

The kids were getting a little spooked, especially after what happened in the Teddy Bear Room. One morning Kristi came to the breakfast table and looked as if she had seen a ghost. "Cindy, all the teddy bears are lined up against the wall." At first I didn't understand why she was so freaked out. Then she told us that she had randomly thrown the bears off the bed and onto the floor the night before.

Lyne loved the Teddy Bear Room and slept there when she came to the ranch. The room was full of teddy bear pictures and there were about 30 different teddy bears of all shapes and sizes that sat on the bed. The kids told me that morning that when Lyne would go to bed she would carefully organize them on the wall in a specific order. A couple of them she turned around to face the wall. She would say things like, "You are best friends with her, and you are married to him" as she lined them up.

When Kristi told us that the bears were lined up on the wall and she didn't do it the kids could hardly eat their breakfast. Some of the bears were even turned around. Had Lyne organized the teddy bears? The girls all started crying and little Jordan had a solemn look on his face.

I looked at all of them, not knowing what to say. I believe now an angel whispered in my ear the words I needed to say to them. "If it had been one of you who died, wouldn't you want us all to know that you were fine and in a beautiful place?" The statement brought peace and understanding to *all* of us.

After that morning when things would fall on their own or light bulbs would flicker and pop we would say things like, "Lyne did it," or "OK, we know it's you, Lyne." It went on like this all summer long. Some would say it was all just our imagination. Who really knows,?? It was real to us!!

Then one day in August, right before the girls went back to their home in Kentucky, Lyne was gone. She loved summers at the ranch and she wasn't going to miss out on this one. How did we know she was gone? We could feel it just as we could feel when she was there.

I have heard that when young people have an untimely death they are not quick to go to the *other side*. Sometimes I can feel Lyne with me now. In my imagination, I can see her skipping beside me with that beautiful radiant smile when I go walking in the woods. The kids all still have their own Lyne experiences as well.

We never *lose* anyone we love. They are always with us because in the spiritual world we are all of the same essence. There is no such thing as *gone forever* because we are immortal spiritual beings. We just change forms.

Love is the language of the soul. When you have a thought about someone you love no matter where their form *is* their spirit always knows that you are communicating love. Have you ever called someone and the person who answers says, "I was just thinking about you." Or maybe you think of someone, the phone rings and it's the person you were thinking of. It happens in the spiritual world as well. If you have a thought about someone who has passed, they are probably sending you love. Just think how happy they would be if you realized this! Wouldn't you?

Whenever I think of someone I love, I acknowledge it and send a love thought to their spirit. I can feel those on the *other side* rejoice when I do. It is always a *Butterfly Moment* when I think of someone who has passed away because somehow I know they are thinking of me as well.

There were many *Butterfly Moments* and lessons learned while living in Texas. However it was time for my *Yellow Brick Road* to lead me into a dark abyss. I had been slowly waking up to my spiritual self and this would serve me well in the hard times that lay ahead.

The river of life was about to hit some turbulent rapids and from this experience I would learn how to completely tune into *The Voice*. When I learned to *really* listen I became aware that danger is just a fear-based illusion. At this point I *believed* this to be true but soon I would *know* for sure.

As they say, "It is always darkest before the dawn."

Cynthia

Peaceful Journey

*"In the middle of the journey of our life
I came to myself within a dark wood
where the straight way was lost."*
—Dante
1265–1321
(The Divine Comedy)

It was 1997 and we were in serious financial trouble. The oil and gas industry can yield great rewards but when you lose, you can lose big too! We were in debt and to top it off our beautiful quarter horses began to literally drop dead. It was a freak condition that occurs every 30 years or so called Dallas grass seed poisoning and within two weeks we lost nine horses.

I am a tree hugger and proud of it. We made the very painful decision to sell the timber on the ranch to pay back taxes. I would never do it again. The acres of beautiful woods that I loved so much now looked like a war zone. What once was a dream had become a horrible nightmare and it seemed that every reason for living on the ranch was gone.

Dennis had made an all-out effort trying to keep everything afloat but we were sinking fast. I had been singing in town but my income was hardly going to make a dent in our seemingly hopeless situation.

My parents still live in the house where I grew up in Redondo Beach and I was there when I received the call. Dennis was in Texas and he sounded so sad. "What do you want to do?"

"I guess it's time to move," I answered.

"California or Nashville?" he asked.

"Nashville."

Nashville, Tennessee was just an hour and a half from where Dennis grew up in Beckton, Kentucky. His father had been a farmer and his mother still lived on the home place. Dennis was practically going home. I, on the other hand, wanted to go where the music was, so Nashville seemed like the best choice.

Adversity is a wonderful teacher. We cannot see the stars during the day when the sun is shining. Only when the night is the darkest, can we appreciate the beauty of the Milky Way. So it is with life. I believe that God allows the darkness so that we can more easily "see the light".

I started looking at things differently. A few days before we left Texas, I remember sitting in my living room looking out the window and seeing the fence outside. Many interesting thoughts floated through my mind: There are many fences. In order for us to inhabit the space inside of the fence that surrounds the ranch, we pay taxes to the county. The county is inside a bigger piece of land called Texas. Texas is inside a bigger piece of land called the United States. The United States is inside a bigger piece of land called North America and all of it is a part of the Planet Earth.

I suddenly realized that we never really owned the ranch. How can you say that you own something that is 4 billion years old and who gave whom the authority to charge us for it? We were paying for permission to borrow the piece of land inside all of the "fences". I was feeling better thinking that you can't lose something you never really owned.

My grandfather always told my dad, "The greatest treasure that a man has is the number of true friends that he can count." This was one of the golden lessons that he learned during the Great Depression. One of the best things you learn when you meet life's challenges is who your friends are.

It so happened that our friends Tommy and JoAnn Strong had their house up for sale in Tennessee where I would come stay with them on my trips to Nashville. They generously gave us a lease option to buy, which meant we had a place to go. I guess you have to experience that feeling of being "homeless" to really understand the meaning of "home".

My brother, Kurt, gave me the best advice I could have heard when he said, "Don't look back!" We were leaving what I knew as "home" under duress and it felt like I was entering the abyss with nothing to guide me but blind faith. There was no choice but to believe that all of this was happening for a very good reason. I kept telling myself, "It is always darkest before the dawn."

I'll never forget the evening we pulled into the driveway of our new "home". Karen, Tommy's daughter, and her husband Larry ran out to greet us. They lived next door and after the long sad drive from Texas it was a heart-touching moment that I shall always remember. I realized as they reached out to welcome us that, although we had left some wonderful friends behind, we were about to make some more wonderful friends.

This new beginning would turn out to be the most exciting phase of my journey. I was becoming more aware of the lessons all around me and, just like a beautiful sunrise the light was subtly showing itself. The events that would take place from this point on would enable me to awaken and finally see the sun.

I remember this one particular moment as if it just happened. It was a beautiful September morning and I was standing in my Tennessee kitchen looking outside. Trees always seem to have silent answers. As I watched the leaves flutter softly in the breeze, it was obvious that they knew much more than me. I wanted to know what they knew. "OK, " I said, "I'm listening."

"Go to Vanderbilt and play songs for the children." It was *The Voice*. I still half thought that The *Voice* might just be my imagination. The Kids for Kids Ministry had taught me that going into *service* is a great cure for depression. Maybe the thought of going to the pediatric ward at Vanderbilt Hospital just seemed like a good idea.

I wanted a different answer. Surely the universe was mistaken! I lived 20 minutes from Nashville, Tennessee, and I had written a number one country song. There was still a catalog of other songs to be pitched. I was expecting something more along the lines of the universe giving me the name of a publisher or producer I should call. My unending optimism and belief in miracles made me think that all of the bad stuff was happening so I could get another hit song.

I found myself trying to argue with *The Voice*. I even went on a couple of music business appointments but nothing was happening. I was getting my answer but it wasn't the one I wanted. It took several weeks of hearing, "Call Vanderbilt," before I finally surrendered to the voice and made a call to their volunteer department.

When I was growing up, my parents had a fun tradition for our birthdays. Mom and Dad would give us a note from the Birthday Turtle. Daddy would make a poem and draw a picture of a turtle on a card. The poem would tell us to go to a location where we would find another note to go to another location. For instance, the Birthday Turtle might say to look under the telephone. Then, under the telephone, would be a note to look under the soap dish in the bathroom. Eventually, all of the notes would lead you to your birthday present. It is a great game that I still play with my children.

When *The Voice* told me to "go to Vanderbilt," it was like the Birthday Turtle game. Vanderbilt Hospital would not be the place I would find my grand prize, but it would lead me to the next place I needed to go.

They did not want me in pediatrics. As it turned out there were plenty of volunteers for sick children. They wanted me to play music in Post-Op where patients were recovering from surgery. I wasn't too keen on the idea but agreed to go along with it. The first day on the job I met a beautiful young woman named Jenny who worked in the Cultural Arts Department. She had long curly black hair and beautiful dark eyes that danced with enthusiasm when she spoke. Jenny walked me around to the different patients and I would attempt to sing them a song or two.

Now the last thing I would want to see in my sick room is "Little Mary Sunshine" with her guitar wanting to sing me a song. In fact, at that time in my life, it would probably annoy me. I found out that there are others who felt the exact same way. Many of the patients rejected the offer and I can't say I blame them.

I tried going back a couple of other times, but the results were pretty much the same and I realized that this was not "my gig". However, there were a few of the patients who really seemed to enjoy the singing and I could see that the music would lift their spirits. Many patients had family members in their rooms and there were a few times when we actually had a little sing-a-long. Volunteering at Vanderbilt taught me that music is *good medicine*.

For the last few years, I had been composing instrumental piano pieces. I would sit at the piano with an image of something and translate the emotion I was feeling into music. Music is made up of numbers and creating music is very much like painting. Consider that every musical tone represents a different color. By finding exquisite combinations, you can create a masterpiece!

Composers use music to express the deepest emotions of the soul just as the artist paints, the dancer dances and the poet writes. It is a gift that reminds us how beautiful and dramatic life is. When their interpretations, touch us deeply and we feel an emotional shudder, I like to call it a *Butterfly Moment*.

Playing classical music had always been my first love. When I was a teenager, I would practice the piano after my family had gone to bed. My parents and my brothers all remember falling to sleep to beautiful soothing pieces like *Swan Lake* and *Moonlight Sonata*.

One evening shortly after my experience at Vanderbilt, Jordan, who was eleven at the time came to me and said, "Mom, would you please play the piano so I can go to sleep?" All of a sudden the bells and whistles started going off and my new mission became crystal clear. I was going to create music to make people relax and feel better.

After my epiphany, it seemed that everything began to fall into place. At first I wasn't sure if I could do it. Up until this point I had always hired musicians but I had never played on any recordings myself. I needed an expert opinion on whether or not I should even attempt the project.

When I first moved to Tennessee I met a woman from Luxembourg named Denise. She was new to town as well. While visiting her home I could see by her CD collection that she had impeccable taste in music. I asked her to come to my home because I wanted her opinion on some compositions I had written. This took a lot of courage because up until now my instrumentals had not been exposed and I knew that Denise would be honest.

As she sat at on the sofa, I played *Behold the Dolphin*. This is a composition I wrote that musically describes an amazing encounter my brother, Mark, and I had in the ocean with four beautiful dolphins. She asked to listen to another and I played *Stonehenge* for her. After a long pause she said, "I will not buy another CD until I buy yours." I took her inspiring words to heart and it was all I needed to get me on my way!

When I finally came to know *The Voice,* and to trust totally in the wisdom and love of the Universe, I saw life in a completely different way. *I began to pay attention!* I no longer tried to *make* things happen, instead I began to *watch* things happen. The more I let go of my illusion of being in charge, the more I saw myself as a participant in a divine plan. *I stopped judging things!* Every invitation was a new opportunity to meet someone who might also be a participant in the plan. No invitation and no person I met was unimportant.

I started practicing and composing every day. When I would finish a new composition I would run next door and play it for Karen. I would invite my new friend, Denise, over to listen to my new creations. One day I was stuck on what to name one of my pieces. I played it for her and asked what it made her think of. "It sounds like sagesse," she said with her beautiful European accent as she fluttered her hands in the air. "It is the French word for "wisdom." I loved the idea and named the piece *Sagesse*.

One day Denise and I had gone to Applebee's for lunch. Our waiter turned out to be a young songwriter named Brad. He told us about a neighborhood bar called Lower Places and invited us to come and hear him sing that evening. The club was named after the Garth Brooks song that says, "*I got friends in Low Places where the whiskey flows and the beer chases my blues away…I'll be OK.*" I had been before and heard some great blues music there, so Denise and I decided to go. It is amazing the number of high quality musicians you can find just about anywhere when you live so close to Nashville, Tennessee.

As I said before, I learned to quit judging, and it's a good thing. Whoever thought that I would find exactly the person I needed to engineer and record my beautiful piano music at a bar named Lower Places??

That night, after his performance, Brad introduced us to his friend. Jerry Webb was a longhaired Texan and he was "country as a sack o' shucks." He also owned a studio here in town.

"Do you have a *real* piano at your studio?" I asked. So many of them use only electric pianos and synthesizers.

"We shor' do," he answered with a grin.

"What kind?"

"We have a K.Kawai at the studio." My heart started beating hard with excitement.

"That's what I play!" The next day I was there.

The Project Room was only five minutes from my house. I met Jerry there and made friends with a beautiful, black K.Kawai grand piano. She had a lovely tone and I instantly fell in love with her.

I had seen Jerry play guitar and I was immediately impressed with his technique and melodic simplicity. I knew that we would work well together. Within a few weeks, I was at the Project Room ready to begin my new musical adventure.

I tried playing a few pieces but I was still feeling a bit insecure and my nervousness was showing up on tape. Jerry has the patience of a saint, and, with his very slow talking Texas accent, he said just the right things to finally set me at ease. We began by communicating in a language that only musicians understand. Then something amazing happened. Jerry and I were communicating on a spiritual level that only the soul understands.

I decided that the way I was going about this was all wrong. If I wanted people to love the music then I had to put love *in* the music. I began to play as if I were in another world. It was like nothing else existed except love, music and my soul. As I played the piano I would fantasize a scenario, bring myself to the deepest emotion of love and then communicate that feeling with my whole being. Sometimes I would go into such a beautiful, loving place that it felt like my body was on automatic pilot. Part of me was playing and part of me was lost in some kind of peaceful bliss.

Jerry could always tell if I had somehow been distracted. I couldn't fool him. Sometimes a foreign thought would slip in about something in the real world and disturb my fantasy. I could play every note perfectly but Jerry would still know because he was that sensitive to the flow of the music. It never ceased to amaze me.

We finished the CD and I named it *Behold the Dolphin*. I drew an abstract picture of two dolphins for the cover and we had 1000 pressed up. It was time to bare my soul to the world.

Denise bought fifty CDs and sent them to her friends in Europe. The reaction was very positive. Sometimes the universe works very fast especially if you are paying attention to *The Voice*.

We finished the CD in April and by May we had a record contract. Dennis had given the CD to a friend, who gave it to his daughter, who worked at a record company. One of the vice presidents walked by and saw it lying on her desk. One thing led to another and before I knew it I was commissioned to finish a series called *The Peaceful Journey* that consisted of four CDs. They also asked for four Christmas CDs and three more for new mothers to play for their babies before and after birth. When the universe gives you an assignment, it doesn't fool around!

This was a great challenge. When I first met Jerry Webb, I only had 5 compositions *completely* finished and now I was looking at doing 11 albums. We don't know what we are truly capable of until we are challenged. Because I knew that my new "assignment" was divine, I completely surrendered to the beautiful creative energy of the Holy Spirit. I had experienced it before with the children's music but I didn't have the awareness then that I had now.

I went to work and didn't look up until it was all finished. From when I first walked into the Project Room in March of 1998 to the last mix in April of 1999 I would end up with 71 original compositions and 126 finished recordings. One musician told me, "Dang...that's a whole dadgum career!" I guess it was.

I was in creative bliss. When you are *on purpose* doing what you love, it is like being in a state of timelessness. I could sit at the piano for hours and have no concept of how much time had passed. That's how you know when you are working on God's time clock.

How did I do it? I listened with complete trust and full attention to *The Voice*. It was time to create that which I was born to be. I invite you now to go into the musical mind of the composer and musician, *Cynthia*.

The Magic Music Well

*"A tone of some world far from ours,
where music and moonlight and feeling are one"*
—Percy Bysshe Shelley
1792–1822
(To Jane: The keen Stars Were Twinkling)

Imagine a beautiful fountain splashing, creating tiny rainbows of color as the water dances in the sunlight. Think of the water as love. When I play the piano, I am like the fountain splashing love on all who hear. The music comes through me just as the water comes through the fountain. When you listen to my music you are listening to love.

Love is the language and true nature of the soul. I use music to communicate love; and so, to the soul, it is familiar. Very often, people will tell me that somehow they feel that they have heard my music somewhere before. When I compose, I visualize myself going to a beautiful well full of cool clear water and dipping into it. I call it *The Magic Music Well*. The water represents love and this is the source of the *Cynthia* music.

Music is made up of numbers and emotion. A great example of this is a kiss. When we give someone a short kiss the emotion is much different than when we make it a long kiss. For instance a "sweet, goodbye kiss" might have one count where a ten-count kiss is altogether different.

Think of your heartbeat. When we run or get excited, the rhythm increases, and when we feel peaceful and calm, the heart beats slowly and steadily. There are endless numbers of rhythms happening all through the universe. The leaves blowing in a breeze, the waves breaking on the sand and the rotation of the earth as it turns on its axis all have their own sense of timing. The universe is an infinite orchestra of life and energy. After all, the word uni-verse means "one song."

Music is sound organized into patterns that express our human emotions. When melodic tones are used in different combinations, the magic of music and its effects are found in the silent space between each note.

It is in this sacred space where we find the emotion and human drama.

In the diatonic musical scale each tone is given a number Do=1 Re=2 Mi=3 Fa=4 Sol=5 La=6 Ti=7 Do=1

In the sixth century BC, a mathematician named Pythagoras first developed this musical number system. Back then the earth was generally believed to be the center of the universe and the number "seven" was considered a sacred number. Beginning with the moon as one, the measure of vibration between the tones of the scale have the same ratio as the measure of the distance between the seven heavenly bodies that were known to man at this time.

Pythagoras saw the whole universe and everything in it as being in "perfect *harmonia*". All things, and the relationship between all things, can be associated and more easily understood with the assignment of numbers. To me, this simply means that the universe is in perfect order and was designed to be harmonic. It is from this beautiful thought that I create music.

As I said before, music is basically made up of numbers and emotion. Based on the C scale, C=1 D=2 E=3 F=4 G=5 A=6 B=7 C=8 D=9 and E=0. Sometimes when I create a composition I start with numbers. The first thing I do is find a group of numbers associated with something or someone I love. I usually use meaningful dates such as weddings and birthdays. I used this method when I created the piece *Atlantis*.

My mother's birthday is 3/7/32. The notes associated with these four numbers are E, B, E, D. I sat at the piano thinking of my mother's beautiful spirit. Although she is warm and generous, there is a part of her that she keeps hidden in mystery. As I played the four notes repeatedly, I thought of my mother's eyes, the mirror to the soul. "Mom is Pisces," I thought as I added a left hand. "Pisces is a water sign... the ocean is water... ah yes...the mystery of *Atlantis*!" Feeling the emotions of love and mystery inspired by my mother's spirit, and visualizing the lost city of *Atlantis*, I went to *the magic music well* and created the music.

Another way that I compose is by starting with some kind of vision and then I musically express my emotion that is attached to what I am envisioning. I used this method when I created *Stonehenge*. My brother, Mark, had given me a small poster of an awesome photo of the Stonehenge that stands proudly in the Salisbury plains of England. I put the picture on the piano in front of me and stared at it with a shift in perception that made it seem real. As I looked deeply into the photograph, I became full of emotion. Although I had not yet been to Europe in this lifetime, the Stonehenge seemed familiar and I felt a sense of grandeur, respect and celebration of life.

I went inside the picture and became spiritually connected with this divine tribute of ancient man to the perfect harmony and order of the universe. I felt myself there in a time, long ago. I felt a sense of sincere ritual and celebration. I could almost hear music and feel a sense of dancing among the giant stones. I began to play my emotion. It was almost as if the composition had already been created and I was just the catalyst of manifestation. I was lost in a timeless moment where all are one with the soul of God.

I remember when I finished *Stonehenge* I played it for Dennis. He looked at me with soulful eyes and said, "I can see the druids dancing around the stones!" Druids? What are druids? I didn't know what a druid was. Dennis did. Somehow I had tapped into another world just one dimension away. My soul had communicated to his soul with music! Just from knowing the title and listening to the music he had a complete understanding and vision in his mind.

Behold the Dolphin is a musical description of an event that my brother, Mark, and I experienced in our hometown, Redondo Beach. It was a *Butterfly Moment* that happened as we were swimming in the ocean early one beautiful July morning. This was truly a gift from the universe. We were treading water in the breakwater as our family sat watching on the beach. Four dolphins that were cruising by patrolling the shoreline actually stopped to play with us.

Musically speaking, this is how the composition came together. The bass line is the constant flow of the ocean as the waves break on the beach. It also represents the dance of the dolphins as they go up and down in the water. At the beginning of the piece, the music describes the distant appearance of their dorsal fins going up and down. Then after we knew they were dolphins swimming towards us, the music changes to the rhythm and beauty of their dance.

When they stopped to play, the dolphins surfed in the waves next to us. It was a beautiful sight. First, they rode the curl and then they did almost a complete circle as they turned back towards the sea. This is described with a cascade of musical tones.

There was a true sense of harmony, mutual respect and love as they circled and swam around us. One of the dolphins was gleefully jumping in the air and they all seemed to be almost giggling like toddlers.

Another one of them even swam under Mark. Here the music becomes filled with tenderness and beauty. Mark and I felt completely in harmony with nature.

Finally, it was time to go our separate ways. In a reverse musical action from the beginning of the piece, we finally say farewell. *Behold the Dolphin* is a tribute honoring man's spiritual aquatic friends.

These are the three basic ways that the composer "*Cynthia*" is inspired to create her music. Now that I felt that I had received a divine assignment, I would use these techniques to accomplish my goals. There is nothing that cannot be achieved when we tap into the loving and creative energy of God.

A Journey In Time

"Time present and time past
Are both perhaps present in time future,
And time future contained in time past"
—T.S. Eliot
1888–1965
(Four Quartets. Burnt Norton)

Imagination is a beautiful gift. With imagination, you can visit medieval castles, the great mysterious pyramids of Egypt, or go back in time to the ancient Celts as they celebrate the mysteries of creation. You can do this at any moment you choose; all you have to do is close your eyes and you are there.

When I created the *Journey In Time* CD, I decided that I would invent a mental time machine. In my mind, I would witness human dramas of the past. I then translated the emotions of my experience to music. When I looked up the word universe, I learned that uni-verse meant one song. I was inspired to write *One Song* as I explored the state of universal time where all becomes one in the *present* moment.

Although I have never visited the pyramids of Egypt, I have always been fascinated with them. They represent so many human conditions. Bondage, grandeur, dreams and spirituality are all interwoven with the construction of the pyramids. In composing *Golden Pyramid*, I wanted to capture these qualities of human experience in the music.

When I closed my eyes, I could see the slaves dragging the huge stones. I became sensitive to the oppression and suffering they must have endured. In music, minor chords have a ring of sadness but they are incredibly beautiful and bring out deep-felt emotion. Using an A minor chord, my left hand began playing a consistent rhythm to musically describe the dragging motion of the big square blocks. The music gives a sense of the slaves' emotionally broken spirit, and the unending physical hardship.

I kept playing the left hand over and over and went deep into my imagination. I saw the slaves struggling under duress. I had images of bondage, despair and back-breaking labor and translated them with music in the bass notes.

I then began to envision a mighty king. With my right hand, I musically described the Pharaoh's desire for grandeur and glory. At the same time, I felt a cold and heartless attitude, having no regard for the human suffering of the tormented slaves. I was filled with awe as I thought of all of the efforts required to fully achieve the manifestation of the great pyramids of Egypt.

All humans have the ability to imagine and dream. I began to think of the slaves' dreams of freedom and the king's dreams of eternal glory. In the middle of the composition, the left hand ceases to play the slave march. Musically, I created a place where the dreams of both royalty and slaves all come together. It is the place where we are one in spirit.

Finally, the end of the piece describes the pyramid in all its magnificence still standing thousands of years later.

Much like the Stonehenge in England, the design of the pyramids gives evidence of the spiritual awareness of ancient man and his understanding of the laws of nature. It is in this spirit that the music of *Golden Pyramid* was created.

With the magic of imagination I hoped that my listener could experience insight into this event in history through music. Creative visualization, along with inspiring music, enables us to become sensitive and aware of all the human passions associated with building the great pyramids in Egypt. The pyramids are a reminder that all of us have the power to manifest our dreams.

A very interesting thing occurred after I recorded *Golden Pyramid*. I gave a copy to a man named Steve who works at the grocery store about a mile from my home. When he is there he always brings out my groceries to the car and we usually have conversations about music.

Steve has a way at looking at the simple things in life in a very beautiful way. I am always happy to see him. A few weeks after giving Steve the CD he made the comment, "I especially loved the *Golden Pyramid*. I could see the slaves pulling the stones." It was a *Butterfly Moment*. I felt a chill run through me as I realized he had heard and understood what I was attempting to communicate with my soul.

As I mentioned before, my father's ancestors are from Scotland and Ireland. It is amazing how our tribal mentality makes us so fascinated with our roots and ancestry. It seems that so many of us almost have a haunting desire to get in touch with our family history and tradition.

Up until then, I had some interest in Celtic tradition. I started doing research on the Celts. The more I learned, the more I wanted to know. I was getting answers to questions I never even knew I had. I was on a journey in time and found that it all seemed very familiar. It was like coming home.

I have a golden friend named Lerin. She is a beautiful girl with long sandy blonde hair and beautiful green eyes. We were born the same year and have known each other since we were teens. My mother used to call us "bookends." My grandmother, Tita, called her "la amiga de la alma" which means "friend of the soul."

Lerin and I met in 1974 at Coco's, where we both worked as waitresses. We became friends because she wanted to learn to play the piano. She had come over one day and asked me to play. When I played the piano for her, she told me that one day I would do great things with my music. I was 19 years old at the time and had no idea what she was talking about. Lerin knew. She has been an inspiration to me ever since.

Now that I had discovered my time machine, it seemed that a whole new world had opened up to me. I wanted to go to the land of the Celts. The best way I knew to do this was with a book.

I called Lerin at her home in New Mexico. "I need a book!" I told her. I knew that Lerin was familiar with Celtic tradition. "I need to go there! I need to smell the smells, taste the food, and experience the Celtic lifestyle. Do you know a book?"

"*Lion of Ireland* by Morgan Llywelyn," Lerin said without hesitation. "I have one here and will send you a copy."

Lion of Ireland is historic fiction filled with the passions of war and romance. The story is about High King Brian Boru, a real man, who ultimately stopped the Viking invasions of Ireland at the Battle of Clontarf in 1015 AD. I got completely lost in the book. It was incredibly well written and I was there. It was like my soul was remembering a lifetime before.

I fell in love with Brian Boru and also with his mysterious love story with Fiona, the druid woman. As I read the book, I could feel his bravery as a warrior and his sensitivity as he played beautiful music on his harp. High on a hill, I saw Kincora, Brian's grand castle on the Shannon River. Morgan Llywelyn's story filled me with inspiration and I began to compose the many emotions I was feeling.

The beautiful and mysterious woman who loved Brian with all of her heart inspired my composition *Fiona*. Brian was Christian and Fiona was a druid. Druidism was described as the "old ways" and the Christians prohibited any marriage between the two. Yet, Fiona would magically appear in Brian's life at times of dismay and heartbreak.

When I wrote *Kincora*, I could see people gathered in the great hall of the castle as Brian sat at the head table, noble and proud. Brian had designed and built Kincora and loved it dearly. He was a sensitive man and appreciated beauty and love. All of these qualities were woven into the music as I created *Kincora*. I imagined listening to Brian playing his harp and wrote *Brian's Harp*.

During the time of Brian Boru, winter was a time of peace because it was too cold to fight. I loved that thought. One day as I was creating *Journey in Time,* I sat at the piano, watching it snow outside my window. It seemed cold and uninviting outside and I began to musically describe the cold, winter day on the piano. I call the composition *Winter Solstice*. I refer to my description as "musical poetry."

Composing *Boru! (Battle of Clontarf)* was very exciting. Morgan Llywelyn describes the great Irish army repeating their war chant "Boru! Boru! Boru!" as they march to battle against the Vikings who had terrorized their land for decades.

The composition begins with the "Boru!" chant. The music sings Boru! Boru! Boru! Boru!

Then a powerful theme begins describing the courage of Brian Boru. It is followed by chaotic music that suggests the battle itself. The music of the fighting accelerates and comes to a climax! It then diminishes back to the war chant. Then there is a long pause.

After the battle, Boru learns that his son and grandson have both been killed. Here the music becomes very sad. Boru is slain while praying in his tent. You can hear the music quietly fading away as the soul does when it quietly leaves the body.

Finally, after putting an end to the Viking invasions of Ireland, *Boru! (Battle of Clontarf)* ends with the war chant. You can almost see the Irish army returning home in bittersweet victory with the body of their High King Brian Boru.

After composing *Journey In Time*, I wrote the author. Morgan Llywelyn, a letter. I told her how much her book had been an inspiration to my compositions.

This was her reply:

Congratulations! Of course I am prejudiced toward the Boru music, which creates such an evocative mood in me. But I like every piece I've heard. I hope the CDs will be available in Ireland. I will urge everyone I know to buy them. Always, Morgan

Of course I was thrilled. We were able to somehow communicate on a spiritual level with her vision of the Brian Boru story and my music. There was a mutual appreciation and perfect balance of creativity.

Sometimes I hear melodies that seem familiar. I have even been moved to tears and gotten "chill bumps." It feels like I have heard these songs in a time before and the music brings a sense of timelessness to the present moment.

I put a medley of some of these haunting Celtic melodies together and named it *In the Spirit of our Ancestors*. It includes *Shenandoah, Danny Boy, Red Is the Rose,* and *Greensleeves*. All of these songs affect my soul deeply.

Music is the language that speaks to our hearts and enhances our emotions. The whole world is full of music! You can hear it all around you if you listen with your heart. With the magic of imagination, music can take you on a journey back in time. It can be an exciting experience. You might even have a *Butterfly Moment*!

Journey of the Dolphin

"I remember the black wharves and the ships,
And the sea tides tossing free
And Spanish sailors with bearded lips,
And the beauty and majesty of the ships,
And the magic of the sea."
—Henry Wadsworth Longfellow
1807–1882
(My Lost Youth)

The ocean is like a beautiful woman. Her cycle is in harmony with the moon and although she can be lovely and serene, she can also be stormy and full of mystery. She is passionate in her emotions. It is always obvious what kind of mood she is in. Listening to her waves breaking on the shore is like listening to the breath of life. Just to look at her endless beauty brings a satisfying peace to the soul.

I grew up in Redondo Beach, California, and although many things have changed since I was a small child, the ocean remains consistently beautiful. At any moment, I can close my eyes and taste and smell her salt, watch a colorful sunset on her horizon, slide down the back of her waves, and hear her ancient song. I know she is always there. She welcomes me with open arms when I come home.

It is in her honor that I wrote *Journey of the Dolphin*. I think of dolphins as friendly ambassadors to mankind. They have saved drowning sailors, protected surfers from sharks and touched us with their magical, healing powers.

I remember a beautiful summer morning when our family had all come together for a family reunion to celebrate my mother's favorite holiday, the fourth of July. It was about 7 o'clock and Daddy had awakened all of us to go for a morning swim.

The ocean lay as still as glass and the sky was bright blue. Ours were the first footprints on the sand, which had been raked perfectly even and smooth. We all ran to the ocean's edge, dropping our towels on the way, and then, one by one, we dove into the shallow surf. The sea was so glassy it was like diving into a pool.

We were all laughing and having a wonderful time. It was a beautiful morning and everyone was happy to be together. After a little while, some of the family started to leave the water and return to the beach. My brother Mark and I decided to linger a bit longer. The ocean was incredibly beautiful and it was difficult to leave her splendor.

I love to get in the breakwater and slide down the back of the waves as they swell and curl. Mark and I were doing this when, all of a sudden, Mark pointed to the right towards Redondo Beach pier and said, "Look!"

At first, I didn't see anything but the pier. Mark always likes to create a little mystery and, with a big grin on his face, he pointed to the right again and said, "Cindy, look!" I looked again. This time I saw four gray dorsal fins going up and down heading our way! My heart started pounding with excitement as I realized there were four dolphins swimming directly towards us.

Mark said, "Put your ears under the water and listen."

Sure enough, we could hear their high-pitched sonar under the water. They were talking to each other! I then went under water and started saying "I love you," over and over again. I had heard that the dolphin had seven folds in its brain and humans only have five. I knew they were masters of communication. I guess I thought they would understand. Mark tried another approach. He started imitating their sound by singing "Bleeeee, Bleeeee, Bleeeee," in a high pitched voice under the water.

Between the two of us, we piqued their curiosity. They decided to stop and play with us. Our family sat on the beach and watched as the dolphins circled around us, jumped in the air, and surfed in the waves beside us. It was a magical, timeless moment and I savored every bit of it.

When dolphins surf in the waves, they do a complete circle so they do not end up on the beach. They do this dance with beautiful grace and style. We were all participating in the harmonious dance of nature. Even now as I tell the story I am filled with awe. Finally, after about twenty minutes, Mark said, "We probably should go in." I was so caught up in this awesome experience that I had completely forgotten our family still up on the beach. In my mind's eye, I can still see all of them watching us from the shore. Those moments were a beautiful gift from Mother Earth and I shall remember them always as a spectacular event in my life.

I thanked the dolphins. Although it seemed I could have stayed in all day, it was time to say goodbye. We swam up to the beach. We could see the dolphins swim away, just as they had come. Their gray backs glistened in the morning sun as they danced up and down in perfect rhythm, as if getting back to their job of patrolling the breakwater. This experience led me to compose *Behold the Dolphin*.

In the Spirit of Dolphins and *Journey with Dolphins* were both composed as tributes to our aquatic mammal friends. In *Journey with Dolphins*, I imagined mighty sailing vessels traveling across the Atlantic with schools of dolphins swimming and dancing all around.

Dolphins seem to be such a friendly breed. They seem to be laughing and singing at the same time and always look like they are smiling. Dolphins seem always playful and love to have a good time. They have wonderful integrity and are always ready to serve. All of these characteristics inspired my composition, *In the Spirit of Dolphins*.

I remember one day, while walking by the beach, I saw people stopping and pointing out towards the ocean to an amazing sight. We saw a baby whale that had lost its way and was heading towards the beach. This could have been fatal for the baby whale. But three dolphins were trying to get it to change its course and head it back out to sea. It was both cute to watch and also fascinating, as the dolphins seemed to be fussing at the baby whale like a nanny would fuss at her charge. The mission ended in success.

I come from a family of dog lovers. We had two dogs that raised us. Charlie was a medium sized brown mixed breed that joined our family when I was 8 years old. He loved to sing when I played the piano. He especially loved the song *Alley Cat*. I can still see him throwing his head back and howling away! He lived 16 years.

After Charlie went to doggy heaven, my brother Steve brought home a German shepherd pup from the pound and named her Daphne. She loved to go with my brother Kurt to the beach. When she passed away Mom and Dad took her ashes and threw them in the ocean.

Now, here is an amazing thing. In all the years while I was growing up in Redondo, we never saw dolphins. It seemed, to us, that right after Daphne's ashes were scattered the dolphins started to show up. Mom jokingly says that Daphne has come back as a dolphin and when she sees dolphins she points and says, "There's Dol-finny!" Since there is no such thing as coincidence, the reincarnation of Daphne, the dog, to Dolfinny, the dolphin, has become a family legend.

I wrote *My Puppy* in honor of Charlie and Daphne. There is nothing cuter than a toddler playing with a puppy. This was my vision as I composed the piece. When you listen to the music you can almost see a puppy sliding across a freshly waxed floor.

For some reason, I associate the ocean with my Latin heritage. *Encantada* is the Spanish word for "enchanted". *Vista Hermosa* means "beautiful view." The Spanish language is soulful and all the Latin languages when spoken are like beautiful music. When I compose music in honor of the sea, I do it with my Spanish heart. It is from there that I am able to express the spirit of deep passions and beauty.

Summer Solstice musically describes summertime and *Vernal Equinox* is my musical interpretation of the new beginnings of spring. These were always my two favorite seasons to play in the ocean.

Widow's Walk was composed a little bit differently than all my other pieces. My parents were visiting from California. I was playing a melody on the piano and Daddy came in and sat on the sofa. "What are you playing?" he asked.

"I don't know, Dad. I have this melody going on here but I don't have a subject. Close your eyes and tell me what you see as I play."

He put his head back with his eyes closed and I played the melody through a couple more times. After a minute or two, he put his head up and said, "I see a widow's walk and a woman looking for her husband lost at sea."

"What's a widow's walk?" I asked.

"It's the walkway on top of houses that are built by the ocean. Remember *The Ghost and Mrs. Muir*? She used to speak to him on the widow's walk." Daddy absolutely loves the sea.

I instantly saw two lovers and I decided to tell their story musically. She has long auburn hair and emerald green eyes. He is a handsome sea captain, muscular and tall in stature, with dark hair and deep blue eyes. He loves her dearly, but the sea is a seductive mistress, calling him to come to her.

At the beginning of my composition, *Widow's Walk,* I play the love theme as they tenderly say goodbye. The young woman stands on top of their home watching as his ship sails off to sea until it disappears over the horizon.

Her spirit is always with him. She has told him to think of her when he looks at the moon. She will do the same. Every night, she paces the widow's walk, looking out to a moonlit ocean anticipating his return.

One night, his ship meets a vicious storm. There are huge waves crashing all around the boat and the situation looks hopeless. The music plays the violence of the storm and then, while maintaining that emotion with the left hand, the right hand plays the love theme. This is to musically describe that, even in the treacherous storm, his one thought is getting back to her. Finally, the storm clears and he heads for home.

Every day and every night she faithfully paces the widow's walk until one glorious afternoon she sees a familiar sight coming in over the horizon. He's home!

Her heart is full of joy! She is there to meet him at the boat dock and they are reunited in a beautiful moment of passion and love. This is the story told by my composition *Widow's Walk.* I just love love!

Of course, the mystery of the lost city of Atlantis has haunted mankind for centuries. According to Plato, Atlantis was a powerful empire and civilization that existed about 9600 BC. Corrupted by power and wealth, the people amassed an army against Greece and Egypt.

Zeus, angered at Atlantis, created floods and earthquakes that sank Atlantis in a night and a day. The story of Atlantis remains one of the great mysteries of all times. It is from that spirit of mystery that I composed *Atlantis*.

SHADOWS IN THE SAND

The ocean has been one of my greatest spiritual teachers. When I swim in the ocean I feel one with the world. Sitting on the beach, I can look out to the horizon and feel a sense of infinite wisdom and eternal beauty. When Buddha was asked, "What is real?" His reply was, "That which never changes." Although the ocean takes on many forms, her spirit is always beautiful.

I have been going to Avenue C beach all of my life. One day as I looked down at my shadow on the sand, I realized that throughout my lifetime, my shadow had reflected many different forms. Yet there was a part of me that had never changed. This is a *silent observer* watching me living my life through my eyes, the *windows* of the soul.

It was an enlightening experience. As I sat on the beach, I contemplated this thought and began to reflect on the beautiful lessons on life and love that the *silent observer* had witnessed. I realized that when love was present, the *silent observer* and I were as one. I began to see images of shadows from times before.

The *silent observer* remembers a shadow on the sand casting the form of Cindy at 3 years old. She is wearing a pink and white gingham bathing suit that has a little skirt. The skirt can be seen in the shadow, as can two long braids that flop about when Cindy runs. Through little Cindy's eyes, the *silent observer* can see a loving mother giving her child a peanut butter and jelly sandwich and a thermos with cold milk. The *silent observer* watches little Cindy play tag with the white, foamy water as the waves wash over the beach.

Next, the *silent observer* remembers a shadow on the sand of Cindy the young girl. Through little Cindy's eyes, it can see her playing with her three brothers and running to the water's edge. A great big man whom Cindy calls "Daddy" takes her out into the surf and lets her hold on to his neck. She laughs with glee as he catches a wave and she rides on his back to the shore.

Then the *silent observer* remembers a shadow on the sand with curves like an hourglass. Through Cindy's eyes it witnesses young men looking at a teenage Cindy with a very different look in their eyes. There are four teenage boys who grab her legs and arms and carry her into the water. She screams and pretends to be indignant but loves the attention.

Now the *silent observer* remembers a shadow on the sand that is now round with child. As a pregnant Cindy sits on the beach, through her eyes the *silent observer* can see her watching the baby's father surfing while new life lightly dances in her womb. The *silent observer* feels Cindy's smile as she responds to her little one by lightly tapping on her tummy.

Finally, the *silent observer* remembers two shadows on the sand. Through Cindy's eyes, it can see a little blonde toddler looking up at Cindy the mother with trusting eyes. Cindy the mother looks at her little girl with pure love as together they play tag with the white, foamy water as it washes over the beach.

The ocean has been a wonderful teacher. It continues to give me *Butterfly Moments* of awareness and when it does, my soul sings and my body is filled with emotion.

Do you have a favorite place that you knew as a child that you know today? In your mind, go there now. Isn't it great! The scenery is basically the same and so is that part of you that never changes.

The Quiet Journey

*"Junah discovered, as Bagger so eloquently put it,
"How to stop thinking without falling asleep".*
—Steven Pressfield
(The Legend of Bagger Vance)

In the beginning, there was God and only God. God is Love. Therefore, in the beginning, there was Love and only Love. God created human beings to discover love. When we finally really know love with no condition, we know God.

Because love is the truest essence of the soul, when we experience love, our souls sing and our bodies react physically. Our hearts feel warm, our solar plexus gets butterflies and, many times, an emotional chill will run through us like a rushing river. Love always feels good because where there is love, there is the presence of God.

Knowing God is an inside job. Just like love, God's voice is silent. To listen to God's voice, we must quiet the mind. We do this by allowing all of the chatter and thoughts to dissipate like wisps of smoke.

I heard someone once say, "Music is in the space between the notes." It is in that space that we can find the silent voice of God. Music is a wonderful way to become "quiet". First, it can take you away from chatter thought to imaginary thought. From there, by listening for the silence in between the notes of the music, you can get to what I call the "peaceful place".

There is no right way or wrong way to meditate. Meditation is simply freeing yourself from thought and going to the place in your mind where there is no-thing. This is your destination. It is from no-thing that every-thing is manifested. I like to call it the big zero.

Remember when you were a little kid in school, and the teacher brought you a fresh piece of paper and a new box of crayons? I can even remember the smell of the crayons. You could put anything you wanted to put on that piece of paper and there was something exciting about having an infinite number of choices. That piece of paper is like the big zero. It is the no-thing from which comes every-thing.

When we create, it is a reflection of ourselves. We see it every day in a child's drawing, a love letter or a meal prepared by a mother to nourish her family. All creation starts with thought and from there it is manifested. When I am creating, it feels like my soul is in complete harmony with the universe.

I created the *Quiet Journey CD* to promote relaxation and tranquility. I know many people who use it for meditation and even some who use it to fall asleep. Funny, I always take that as a compliment.

The compositions on *Quiet Journey* are all expressions of peaceful thoughts and emotions. The music is relaxing and maintains a consistent easy flow. So many people seem to be looking for ways to find peace and tranquility in their lives. It is from peace and tranquility that this music was created. As a result, the peace and love I experienced in the creation of this music, spills onto the listener like the water from a fountain.

I'd like to share those things that inspired the music for Quiet Journey.

Located in the Grand Canyon in the high desert, is the magical city of Sedona, Arizona. It is a beautiful place with red, desert scenery and mystical ambience. For centuries the Native Americans have considered it sacred ground. Sedona is believed to have "magical earth energy," because of seven vortexes that meet in its location. A vortex is to the earth as the heart is to the body. It is a location where there is a strong energy source. Ancient stone circles, including Stonehenge, are built on these types of locations. This tells us that our human ancestors had an acute awareness and sensitivity to our beautiful earth. Sedona is my musical expression of mystical beauty.

I met Santiago in Lake Cherokee, Texas. He was of Native American decent and he had a beautiful spirit. His sad eyes seemed to represent the oppression of his ancestors. I instantly was full of compassion and love for this man. After spending hours talking with him, I was full of inspiration. I sat at a piano and began playing. "This is you," I said as I played.

His dark eyes filled with tears and he said, "Oh no. The music is too beautiful and I am not beautiful." I told him he was one of the most beautiful souls I had ever met. Within a few minutes, Santiago was created. It was a spiritual experience I shall always remember.

Baby Horse was written when I lived in Texas. I was sitting at the piano and saw a new foal nursing on its mother. I especially remember the rhythm of the mare's tail, swishing back and forth in pure contentment. I incorporated this rhythm in the piece. It was one of those beautiful and tranquil moments where all of nature seems to be in perfect harmony.

Music is like poetry. Every language has its own music and when we want to emphasize emotion we speak louder, softer, faster and slower. Our tones change as well. For instance when I get excited, my pitch goes up. Music is exactly the same. In musical language, when I want to enhance my statement, I give the note a long pause. It is in the silence that we can hear the eternal, silent voice of God. This is where all the magic is. Every answer to any question can be found in the silence.

I have a beautiful friend, Elaine, who sees the world with spiritual eyes. She is wonderful with words and we have written several songs together. Elaine wrote this lovely poem and her imagery inspired me to create the music to *Shadow Dancer*.

SHADOW DANCER
—Elaine Benedict

*As silent as a moonbeam falls…love calls,
the dreamer answers.
And reaching for that flaming heart
becomes a shadow dancer.*

Quiet Journey, Quiet Within and *Serena* were all composed from that very peaceful place that I experience when I meditate. The word "serena" means serenity. Now, whenever I listen to these pieces I go to my peaceful place instantly. Meditation takes me to a place that feels safe and secure, where the only presence is love. I become like a drop of seawater reuniting with an endless ocean of magical dreams.

I have always thought that ancient man had a different kind of knowledge and understanding of the universe than we do today. The ancients saw the sun as a god and believed that it was actually the creator of the world. The ancients were thankful and grateful to the sun for the gifts of light, warmth and nourishment to the earth. It is in the celebration of these gifts that I composed *Sundance*.

A GREAT HYMN TO THE ATEN
1350 BC

Earth brighten when you dawn in lightland
When you shine as Aten of daytime
As you dispel the dark
As you cast your rays
The two lands are in festivity
Awake they stand on their feet
You have roused them

When I was in high school I read the book *Jonathan Livingston Seagull* by Richard Bach. It is a story that teaches there are no limits to how high we can fly. I composed *Eagle Star* with this story in mind. I imagined a beautiful eagle soaring higher and higher among the stars. As I created the piece, I felt a gentle sense of freedom. Freedom is the nature of the soul. When we finally *remember* that freedom is our true nature all forms of bondage disappear. No matter what life dictates, our souls are always free to love and be one with all that is. When we realize that love and freedom is what we are all about, the soul sings in celebration of life.

The autumnal equinox is the day between summer and winter when the light hours and dark hours are equal in length. It introduces the fall season. We have a lot of beautiful trees in the yard and I composed *Autumn Equinox* one day as I witnessed the leaves falling and blowing in the wind.

There is a Native American legend that tells why the leaves change to brilliant beautiful colors in the fall. It seems that at one time, all trees were green. Some of them were jealous of the pretty colors of the wild flowers that grew in the fields.

The trees came to Earth Mother and complained. "We want to have beautiful colors like the flowers," they said. With a voice filled with love, Earth Mother replied, " But that's not your true self. You are precious just the way you are."

"We want to be like *them*!" said the unhappy trees.

Earth Mother agreed to grant their request, but, she said, because of their vanity, there would be a price to pay.

"We don't care," said the trees. "Just change us to the pretty colors."

It was just after summer. Earth Mother, with her amazing wisdom and magical powers, granted the trees their wish. They began to turn beautiful colors of yellow, orange, red and even bright fuschia. They were so happy! They were showing off to the trees who decided to remain green. "We are beautiful and you are still that boring green," they taunted.

They bragged and boasted for only a few weeks and then suddenly the vain trees began to lose their beautiful leaves. Winter was approaching and there they stood with naked branches. They began to cry. "We want to be like we were!" they wailed.

Earth Mother took pity on her children and restored their green leaves again in the spring. However, every autumn the trees become beautiful again with fall foliage. Then, as a reminder of their vanity, they lose their leaves in the winter and become barren. Earth Mother blessed the trees who remained true to their identity and called them "evergreens."

I just love this story!

All of my compositions are like my children. However, once in a while, a feeling of love comes through me that is so incredibly deep that I cannot put it into words. This describes my composition *First Light of Dawn*. It is symbolic of enlightenment, new beginnings and love so powerful that it can change your life forever. When I recorded *First Light of*

Dawn, I played it end to end without fixing or changing a note. This is unusual for a song that is almost 7 minutes long. I was in a complete state of timelessness and bliss.

Every time I hear my recording of *First Light of Dawn*, it has an anchoring effect on me that returns me to that blissful state of love. I can feel the emotion run through me like a rushing river. What is amazing is that this piece has stood out to others as well.

I have a beautiful friend named Jo Ellen who is surviving a bout with cancer. I am very proud of her because she has outlived the doctor's prognosis of her disease. Jo Ellen is an apprentice to my dear friend Sally. They share an office where they practice hypnotherapy. Sally and Jo are part of a group of friends who all come to my home on Wednesdays for spiritual conversation. We call our group "The Circle of Sacred Knowing."

One day I was in Sally's office and I could hear Jo crying in the next room. Her pain was intense and Sally ran in to tend to her. The next thing I knew I was listening to the *First Light of Dawn* playing. In a very short time, the crying stopped. The song repeated over and over. Jo was not aware I was there. I found out from Sally that when she hears this particular piece, it actually makes her feel better. Now I was the one with tears, as I realized that I had learned how to listen to God's silent voice. It was not my imagination. God was using me to promote healing with music.

I think of music as poetry and poetry as music. The inspiration for this poem came to me early one winter morning as I sat and watched a beautiful, quiet sunrise.

The First Light of Dawn
—Cynthia Jordan

It is the darkest hour.
You can hear the silent voice of the night
as the land waits patiently for her arrival.
She will come… She always does.
Quietly at first, the sweet songs
of small-feathered minstrels fill the air
as if announcing, "Her Majesty is approaching!"
From the east a soft glow of light can be seen on the horizon.
Then, subtly, before all who have the privilege to witness,
the sky is transformed into an exquisite masterpiece!
The lady, being quite the lady,
very slowly reveals her beauty with grace and style.
Bright magentas and brilliant colors of fiery orange
and gold exhibit her passions as she paints a
magnificent picture of endless beauty!!
My breath is taken away… She is here!
Her heavenly essence seeks no approval
as she generously lights the new day, a new beginning for all.
She is not selective and gives unconditionally
as she embraces all of life with her warmth and light.
Her lovely golden rays shimmer through the forest trees
and shine boldly through the clouds.
A gentle peace fills my soul at the First Light of Dawn.

The Celtic Journey

"Of all the trees that grow so fair,
Old England to adorn
Greater are none beneath the sun
Than oak, and ash and thorn"
—Rudyard Kipling
1865–1936
(A Tree Song)

It is May first. The green has returned to the land after a long cold winter. The trees are in bud and new flowers decorate the fields with beautiful colors. The season of growth, it is time for farmers to follow their herds to higher pastures for summer grazing.

The days have become longer. There is a soft breeze blowing through the land singing the song of spring. The crops have been planted and it is a time to celebrate the fertility and blessings of our beautiful Mother Earth. All are gathered in a clearing in the woods and you can hear music, singing, and laughter as the Clan dances around the fire.

The smell of burning oak branches fills the air and all are feasting in merriment. The children hold long strands of ribbons as they dance and weave around the "Maypole." It is the grand festival of Beltaine.

Young lovers present themselves to the Clan as man and wife and then steal away into the forest to consummate their union. Other couples join in this ritual to renew their commitment to each other. All joyfully celebrate the mystical miracles of life!

Again, it was time to take a trip in my mental time machine. I began reading books about the Celts. The more I read the more I wanted to read. About this time, my daughter Julie took me on a trip to Italy. On the plane I read *The Druids* by Morgan Llywelyn. It is a historical novel set when Julius Caesar had begun his conquests and disrupted the Celtic way of life.

As I read, I could smell the intoxicating aroma of smoke filling the air as pieces of oak trees burned in the fire. I felt cool earth on my bare feet and could taste the sweet wine so carefully made from the grapes in the vineyard. As we were landing in Rome I looked at Julie and said, "Strange, but it feels like I've come home."

When I returned from Italy, I spent three days lost in time. I wrote one composition after the other as I musically told the story of the amazing Celts and their celebrations of life. It was probably the three most prolific days I have ever had creating music.

For many years, I have played my guitar for small events and happy hours. One of my favorite songs to sing is *Shenandoah*. I later found out that the Shenandoah Valley in Virginia was named after the Shannon River in Ireland. The beautiful green landscape and scenery around the river reminded the early Irish immigrants of their homeland in Ireland.

I used to sing at Lee Wright's in Shreveport, Louisiana. My friend Fred Sexton, who we all call "the judge," used to request *Shenandoah* every night. It was one of those songs that would put me in a trance. I would close my eyes and see a very vivid picture of a beautiful river with green and misty hills all around.

The Shannon is a composition that describes this image musically. The left hand plays a flowing water motion as the right hand plays a tender melody. To me, the song of a river is like an ancient lullaby. In the middle of the piece I combine the flowing music of the left hand with the *Too-Ra-Loo-Ra* lullaby in the right hand. It always makes me think of my Irish grandmother, Moe.

The oak groves were considered sacred ground to the Celtic druid priests. It was here that they practiced their religious rituals, designed to send magical energy to their crops and to warriors in battle. The druids were very secretive. It took about 20 years to become a druid priest. There were thousands of verses to learn as well as magic and mystic rituals. As I composed *Oak Forest*, I could feel the sacred mystery of the oak groves.

Mistletoe is symbolic of fertility and friendship. The Celts would display mistletoe on the window sills and doors of their homes to let weary travelers know they could stop for food and lodging. If two enemies should meet under an oak with mistletoe growing on it, the honorable gesture was for both to lay their swords down for 48 hours, which was enough time to cool off. The Celts call mistletoe "oak child" because the best form of the herb grew on the sacred oak. These beliefs inspired the lighthearted melody *Oak Child,* which, on my Christmas CD, is named *Mistletoe.*

The ancient Celts saw the elements of nature as very sacred. Archeologists have found evidence that precious artifacts from the Iron Age, with elaborate designs of circles and curves, were thrown as offerings into the rivers. Some claim that this is the origin of the wishing well. When I composed *Wishing Well,* I imagined people, especially children, making wishes and throwing their coins.

In Celtic tradition, music plays a significant role. The bards (musicians) wrote songs to pass on stories of heroism and folklore. The "Seanchai." is the name given to the storyteller, the historian. He would visit homes and meeting places to tell historical tales from times past. The Celts did not write stories down. They relied on the bards and the storytellers to keep history alive. This tradition lasted for centuries.

When I composed *Seanchai* I imagined a man, with a long robe and beard, sitting in a family lodge by a fire, telling a tale after the evening meal. I felt that the story was humorous and you can even hear laughter in the music.

I composed *Fireside* with that same imagery of family and friends sitting beside a warm fire as the golden glow fills the room with soft light. The feeling is that of peaceful contentment, which is expressed in the music.

There is a beautiful place in the Highlands of Scotland known as The Great Glen. Although I have never been there, when I read about it, a scene instantly came to my mind. I could see a young lass picking wild flowers and singing a lovely tune as she put them into her basket.

High on a hill is a nobleman on a white steed watching her. He is completely enamored by her beauty. She has long beautiful brown curly hair and hazel eyes that dance in the sun. They fall in love and live happily ever after. This imaginary love story inspired the music of *The Great Glen*. (I'll admit that I am a romantic.)

I was fascinated to learn how many Celtic traditions we still practice today. Beltaine and Samhaim are the two main festivals celebrated by the Celts. In the spirit of these festivities, I composed *Celebration of Life*! I could see people dancing to flute music, singing songs and drinking wine.

As mentioned earlier, Beltaine is the celebration of fertility and new life. For the Celts it marks the beginning of summer season. Today we know it as May Day. The "maypole" is decorated with long strands of bright colored ribbons. The children each take a ribbon end and the strands are woven together as the children sing and dance around.

Samhaim is the festival that marks the beginning of winter. This was the greatest festival on the calendar and signified the new year. The Celts were extremely superstitious and believed that they could ward off evil spirits by wearing scary masks. Samhaim was celebrated around huge bonfires. Sound familiar? It is celebrated today as Halloween. I composed *Samhaim* with an air of sacred mystery in the music, in the spirit of this very important Celtic festival also known as All Hallows Eve (Halloween).

When I composed *A Mother's Heart* and *Homeland* I felt a sense of loyalty, love and home. Both of these pieces embrace these tender and heart-warming emotions. The Celts were very passionate and I love to tell their story musically.

The early Celts resided mainly in what we know today as Switzerland and France. The soldiers of the Roman Empire drove them to the north and across the water. They settled in what are now known as Ireland, North England, Scotland and Wales, all of which still retain signs of their ancient Celtic heritage. How sad it must have been for the early Celts to leave their beloved homeland. This made me think of our ancestors coming to America. The very sensitive *Emerald Valley* musically describes the love I have for my Irish heritage.

All of the music for the Celtic CD had been composed. I had smelt the smoke, felt the earth and tasted the wine. It all seemed familiar to me and I felt like I had come home. Was I getting information from a past life or was all of this just my imagination? Why did some Celtic music seem so familiar that I actually experienced a physical rush? Was my fantasy that real or was my soul remembering emotions from a time long ago?

I guess it didn't really matter. It was a beautiful experience that I relive every time I play or listen to the Celtic music I composed. However, there is one thing that happened that might serve as a clue that this was not simply my imagination.

When I was in the fourth grade, our music teacher taught us a song called *The Ash Grove*. I remember hearing it for the first time and falling in love with it. Our songbook had illustrations and I always found myself turning to *The Ash Grove* page to stare at the picture. It was one of my favorite songs and I loved when we sang it.

When I put together my Celtic CD, I had a feeling that I should record *The Ash Grove*. I don't know why exactly, I just felt very strongly that the song should be on the album. I did a light piano arrangement and Jim Unger laid a beautiful violin track on it.

After turning the finished masters in to the record company I received a call from Cassandra, who was in charge of product development. "Rick doesn't want *The Ash Grove* on the CD."

I felt a sense of panic. "Why?" I asked.

"He only wants original material," she answered.

Irritated, I found myself insisting that *The Ash Grove* be kept on. "What difference does it make??' I exclaimed. "The song is PD (public domain) and he doesn't have to pay royalties! I don't understand why it can't be on the CD?"

This was weird. I didn't even know why I was upset. It was just one song. I guess it was because I thought *The Voice* had told me to record *The Ash Grove*. Cassandra sensed my panic and finally said, "Ah, don't worry about it. As long as it's PD it will be fine." Whew...I felt relieved.

I think that God gives us little stumbles to get our attention and make a point. Otherwise, we might miss the lesson. About six months after *Celtic Journey* was released in the stores I was reading a book that explains all kinds of facts on Celtic rituals and beliefs.

I opened the book to the music section and as I was looking through the songs, I came upon a song called *Llweyn On*. Under the title of the song was written "Englyn for Beltane". The sheet music was familiar. When I read the caption below a chill ran through me and I could feel my heart jump.

The caption read: " Known in popular form as THE ASH GROVE, this lively song is meant to reflect the babbling brooks, the new-green leaves, and dance of summer breezes."

Coincidence? Maybe. Personally, I don't believe in coincidences. I do however believe in *Butterfly Moments* and the way I see it, God was letting me know that the whole *Celtic Journey* experience was not my imagination.

About a year after the release of the *Peaceful Journey Series* Lerin and I took a trip to Europe. We visited Chartres, France, home of a magnificent cathedral that was built in the twelfth century AD. It is the Notre Dame Cathedral of Chartres, and it stands tall and proud on the site of one of the most sacred oak groves known to the Celts. After their Christian conversion, this was a way to bridge the two religious beliefs.

On the floor, inside the cathedral, is a large circle with a labyrinth design. The design inside the circle is a painted geometric path that creates a circular pattern. The labyrinth has been used for centuries as a form of prayer and meditation. Even today, pilgrims come from all over the world to walk the labyrinth at the Cathedral in Chartres.

Of course, the cathedral is a magnificent early Gothic structure. It has a very impressive history and grandeur, including its world famous, beautiful stained glass windows.

As I was walking outside the cathedral I saw something that also impressed me. There, growing on the outside walls of the church about 30 to 40 feet above the ground were beautiful bouquets of yellow wild flowers thrust from the stones. It was amazing! How did the seeds get up there and how were the flowers taking root?

Suddenly, it occurred to me that Mother Earth has everything under control. Somehow, man has developed the illusion that he's in charge! There is even talk that we have the power to destroy the earth. How egotistical to think we have that kind of power.

Man might be stupid enough to destroy his environment and even mankind's existence but he does not have power over universal intelligence. After all, Mother Earth is at least 4 billion years old and man has only been around 250 million years or so. There is no telling what she has already survived.

The precious, yellow flowers reminded me that the loving hand of the Creator replenishes nature's harmony every single day. It made me smile. I then walked over and started hugging the trees trying to imagine the beautiful, sacred oak grove that stood there many hundreds of years before. Yes, I'm a tree hugger.

We can learn much from the Celts. They had an acute understanding of nature and celebrated in thanksgiving its beauty and many wonderful gifts. It is an honor to translate the Celtic story to beautiful music.

New Beginnings

"Every moment is a new beginning."
—Cynthia

Life is a miracle and a beautiful gift. It is precious to the soul because without life's experience the soul cannot know itself. When we are aware and feel the presence of unconditional love, the soul sings in harmony with the whole universe, *"This is love! This is what I am!"*

There are only two emotional elements in life. They are love and fear. Love is the nature of the soul. It is the presence of God felt only in our hearts. Fear is the nature of our human ego. It is the absence of God and fools us with false illusions.

Every time a baby is conceived, it is a new opportunity for the soul to have a brand new human experience. We are God's exquisite design because we have the gift of awareness. God has also given us the freedom of choice, and love is always the best choice.

It was April 11, 1972. My mother took me to the doctor. I was seventeen years old, a senior in high school. I was also a CCD second grade teacher at the church. The children had just made their First Communion and I had a class that afternoon.

The feminine products no longer disappeared under the bathroom sink and my mother was suspicious. It was my first female examination and I didn't like it. I wasn't even sure why Mom had brought me. I was one of the very naïve teenage girls, in complete denial. Steve and I had been high school sweethearts for two years. My friends were all "doing it" and I was telling myself, "It won't happen to me".

The doctor felt around and he said, "I can feel the uterus is full. Close to three months I would say." My mother was waiting in a room outside.

The doctor told me to get dressed and meet me in his office. He left the room and as I sat there on the table I could hear a tiny, tiny little voice saying, "Mommy." It began to repeat over and over. "Mommy, Mommy, Mommy." I was going to have a baby.

I put my school uniform back on and went into the doctor's office. I kept hearing that little voice, "Mommy." The doctor had an appointment book out and he was flipping through it.

"How old are you?"

"I am 17."

"When will you be 18?"

"May fourth," I answered.

"Your mother doesn't have to know. I'll just tell her that you need a D and C. We can do it this weekend," he replied.

What was he saying? An abortion! The little voice kept calling to me. Motherhood wasn't exactly what I had in my plans. Come to think of it, I didn't really have definite plans. I just assumed that I would go to college. All these thoughts were racing in my head but above all I could hear, "Mommy."

"Call my mother in," I said.

"Are you sure?" he asked. He didn't like my answer.

"Yes."

He sighed, shrugged his shoulders and said, "OK."

The best choice I could have made! Six months later I would give birth to a beautiful 8lb. 2oz baby girl. Even to this day Julie Lynn still calls me "Mommy."

There is nothing like the feeling of life growing inside you. I remember the first time I felt Julie kick. It was as quiet and soft as a butterfly wing. Nurturing new life is the greatest blessing and experience of womanhood. Pregnancy is our female sisterhood. Every time I see a pregnant woman it makes me smile. Without saying a word I know exactly what the woman is experiencing. I love to watch them rub their tummies.

When the record company asked me to do three CDs for expectant mothers I was very excited. I decided to musically share my own experience of pregnancy, as only a woman can.

Julie Lynn speaks Italian, French, and Spanish fluently, and gets by well in German; and manages a little Portuguese. She just started learning Russian. She claims that learning languages comes easily to her because of all of the music she heard growing up, as well as while she was in *utero*. While pregnant with Julie, I was still practicing every day and taking piano lessons from Dr. Albanese. Julie says that each language has its own music. It's just a matter of filling in the right words.

In the book the *Mozart Effect*, the author, Don Campbell, says, "the fetus really does begin to hear sounds from the outside world between the third and fourth months of development." Music is the universal language. New life responds as the soul recognizes the harmonics of the music. I know that while in the womb, my little babies all had reactions to music. It seemed that the more lively the songs, the more movement I could feel. When I listened to more soothing, relaxing pieces, I could feel my baby's sense of contentment.

Music can serve as an anchor. Have you ever heard a song that reminds you of someone? When you hear it, you instantly think of that person and feel the emotional attachment that you have with him or her. With this in mind, it makes perfect sense that when a baby hears music that it associates with the safety and warmth of the womb, it becomes content.

It has been proven that even years later, children will recognize music that was played to them while *in utero*. My daughter Denise proved to me that this is true.

When I assembled the music for *New Beginnings,* I decided to make it a combination of original compositions, new arrangements of traditional children's songs, and favorite classical pieces that I love to play. The three CDs would promote different musical atmospheres. We named the CDs *Our Miracle, Our Playtime* and *Our Sleepytime*. The selections for each CD were chosen according to the title's theme.

My daughter, Denise, likes to study to my piano music and she has all of my recordings. One day, she came into me and said, "Mom, every time I hear this one piece, I find myself playing it over and over again, sometimes eight or ten times. I really love it." "Which one?" I asked. She played it for me and I realized it was *A Mother's Heart*.

What was amazing is the fact that she picked this one piece out of all the *Peaceful Journey* original compositions, as well as the *New Beginnings*.

There were 71 to choose from and she named this one—with no solicitation.

She was fourteen years old at the time. Somehow, all these years later, she had recognized this one melody. I realized that it was the *only* instrumental that I had written and played before she was born. I had composed it around 1982 when I was still living in California. I was having a *Butterfly Moment*. It literally blew me away!

This was a great project and I was into it. I took the numbers of Denise's birthday, 9/16/1985 and wrote *September's Child*. The composition is my musical expression of her spirit. I thought of her sweet disposition and soulfully, beautiful eyes as I created this piece.

Mommy's Baby was written with the numbers of Julie's birthday. My mother had picked Julie Lynn as the girl's name for all three of my brothers. My daughter was named for the little sister I never had. Even now I still call her "Mommy's baby."

Going Fishing With Papa is my musical interpretation of watching Daddy and my son, Jordan, walking with their poles to the pond on the ranch in Texas to fish. In the music you can see them casting their lines. The whole piece is a great visual.

I love Winnie the Pooh! All of my children had Winnie the Pooh blankets, outfits, stuffed animals, mobiles, and pictures on the wall. Sears loved me! I wrote *Preparing the Nursery* from my experience of baby showers and shopping for my new baby's room. It reflects our maternal need to prepare the nest and it was great fun.

As I was composing *New Beginnings,* I found out my friend Jenny from the Vanderbilt Cultural Arts Department was expecting a baby. She had a beautiful glow all around her and I remember the way she lovingly rubbed her tummy when I'd see her. *Jenny's Due Date* is written from the numbers of the date her little girl was expected to arrive.

The classical pieces I chose are selections I like to play when I feel stressed or anxious. They include *Moonlight Sonata, Adagio Cantabile, The Swan, Brahm's Lullaby, To A Wild Rose and Minuet in G.* I also included Schuman's *The Happy Farmer.* It is one of the musical themes in the

Wizard of Oz and one of my all time favorites, without a doubt.

I created original arrangements of familiar children's songs that I knew myself as a child and that I have taught my children. They are songs like *Mary Had A Little Lamb, Songs I Learned In Kindergarten* and, of course, *Greensleeves*. They are all done in *Cynthia* style.

One day as Jerry and I were recording *New Beginnings*, I was sitting at the piano and I asked Jerry, "Would you like to hear what it feels like the first time you feel your baby kick?" Without writing anything down, I played about a minute's worth of my musical interpretation of that *First Little Kick*. Jerry recorded it on the spot.

Feeling new life as it grows inside of you is the most spiritual experience I have ever had the privilege to experience. There is nothing to me more beautiful than a mother with her new baby. Nursing my babies was the most content and peaceful feeling I have ever experienced. I wrote *Our Miracle* from this complete state of bliss.

This Time Next Year and *You're Going To Be A Mother* were composed from those little fantasies and daydreams I would have while pregnant with my children. I used to love to go to the baby sections of stores and just look around. I would pick up little tiny shoes and clothing with a feeling of happy anticipation. I wove the melody *Twinkle Twinkle Little Star* into *This Time Next Year* to express the anticipation of singing to my new baby.

Balloons, Chasing Butterflies, Dancing Teddy Bears and *Ice Cream Cones* were all written with pictures in my mind based on some of my favorite memories of my children when they were small.

Watching life through a child's eyes is a beautiful experience. My children have been and continue to be my greatest teachers. These are lovely *Butterfly Moments* that I deeply cherish.

A Time of Peace

"Peace on the earth, good will to men
From heav'n's all gracious king
The world in solemn stillness lay
To hear the angels sing"
—Edmund Hamilton Sears
1810–1876
(It Came Upon A Midnight Clear)

Christmas is a time of Peace. No one really knows the exact date that Jesus was born. I always assumed it was December 25 in the year one. In my research, I learned some interesting facts about the history of Christmas.

It is important to remember the circumstances of the time that Jesus of Nazareth was born. There were no calendars or printing presses, as we have today. Most people could neither read nor write. All religious text was written by hand and stored in the temples. Because of human tyranny, many of the records were destroyed and burned. Everything we know about Jesus is from his teachings as passed orally on. Nothing was written down until after his death and the Bible wasn't written until 325AD.

During the early days of Christianity, the Romans worshipped many gods. They had great reverence for the sun god, Apollo. His feast day was December 25. It was a celebration of the blessings of the sun after the winter solstice. There were huge festivals and celebrations going on throughout the Roman Empire.

The friends and followers of Jesus of Nazareth were widely considered to be a rebellious sect of Jews. They gathered in secret meeting places to avoid persecution. The early Christians chose December 25 to honor the birth of Jesus. In this way, they could celebrate freely without attracting attention to themselves.

Christmas is a time of peace. Throughout history, all wars and feuds were put on hold during the winter months. The message of Jesus is all about giving, forgiving, peace and love. This is the spirit of Christmas.

From this spirit, I created the four Cynthia Christmas CDs. *Toyland Christmas* has Santa Claus songs, *Shepherds and Angels* is full of angel songs and *Celtic Christmas* has traditional Christmas music. The *Christmas Celebration* CD musically tells the Christmas story in chronological order.

Christmas standards have been recorded thousands of times. My greatest challenge was to arrange and produce these timeless songs as they have never been heard before. I was fortunate to find excellent musicians and their creative spirit had no limits. I would tell them what I had in mind and they made suggestions as well.

An amazing thing about Nashville musicians is that many of the best ones don't even read music. They play from the number system, created by Pythagoras in the sixth century BC, as discussed earlier. All they need is the numbers. The magic comes straight through their souls.

Musicians communicate in terms of the *feel* of the composition. I would suggest an image or emotion and they knew exactly what to do. They just followed the numbers and perfectly complemented the piano tracks I had already laid down. It was amazing and the results were beautiful!

Jim Unger played violin, John played cello, Wendy played the harp, Charlie played stand-up bass and Jerry played guitar. We had a woodwind master named Sam who brought about 60 instruments. He had flutes of all sizes and did some great things with the oboe as well.

It was an honor to watch and listen as these amazing musicians created their contributions right on the spot. It was as if the music had pulled them into that special creative dimension where all are in harmony with the universe.

Most of the Christmas music consisted of standard tunes that we all know and love. I wrote one composition called *No Room At the Inn*, which musically tells the story of Mary and Joseph trying to find lodging in Bethlehem. In the music, you can hear Joseph trudging along with frustration. His wife is in labor and twice the innkeepers reject him. When he asks an innkeeper the third time you can hear a change in the music as he is finally is sent to a stable in the back.

I told the violinist, Jim, to be the voice of Joseph, and Sam, who played flute, to be the voice of Mary. They did some amazing things with the music and you can hear all of the emotions of Mary and Joseph through flute and violin. The cello stayed steady and sure, just like the donkey.

When I recorded *Silent Night,* the beginning of the song uses just one note. I wanted to musically give the illusion of silence without being completely quiet. I did it several times before we finally got it on tape. It is tricky to capture emotion when playing just one note.

I wrote *Shepherds and Angels* by going back in my mental time machine and seeing the angels appearing to the shepherds on the hills. I played the piano as if it was a beautiful angel harp instead of the giant harp with hammers that it actually is.

I call *Joseph's Dream* the "pancake song". There were many scrambled eggs and pancake dinners while I worked on my CDs. I was trying to be a mom, composer, musician, wife and domestic goddess all at the same time and sometimes my roles would take up the same space. I had just poured pancake batter on the grill when I got the idea for *Joseph's Dream* and ran to the piano to play the melody singing in my head. After I don't know how long, my hungry son came in and said, "Mom, don't you think you should turn those pancakes?"

"Oh my gosh!!" I had completely forgotten!

Needless to say, the pancakes were very dark, so I made some more.

I love to listen to the Christmas CDs. The music all came together in beautiful harmony with each instrument making its unique contribution to make it work together.

I wrote the Christmas music arrangements in 1999. This would turn out to be a Christmas of enlightenment. Jordan is my Christmas baby, the most wonderful Christmas present I've ever had. Jordan's birthday is December 17, and he was just turning 13.

My son is a very clever young man. As the only boy with five older sisters, he has become a master of manipulation. He was obviously concerned that Santa wasn't going to come that Christmas. Up until then, he always had before.

Jordan had obviously figured out the Santa Claus thing quite some time before, but he was playing his part to the hilt. "Gee, I wonder what Santa is going to bring me this year? Mom, don't forget to get carrots for the reindeer. Boy, I just can't wait for Santa Claus!"

Like many of us Peter Pan thinkers, he just wasn't ready to grow up. But the facts were, this was a boy who was growing hair under his arms and squeaking every now and then when he talked. It was definitely time to lay the facts on the table.

Yes, the *moment* had arrived. This is one of those crucial turning points in parenting that you have to face the music and 'fess up to the real truth about Santa Claus. It was definitely time or, knowing Jordan, this little act would probably go on another 50 or 60 years. Handling my truth-loving Sagittarian child was going to be a challenge. How do you explain Santa Claus without coming off as being a betrayer of the truth?

Every moment of inspiration ("in-spirit"-ation) is a *Butterfly Moment* and I was having one now. "Jordan," I said, "There are three phases of Santa Claus."

Phase one: you hear the story when you are small. This story is different all over the world. Ours is the one with the North Pole, elves, sleds and reindeer. On Christmas Eve, we put out cookies and milk for Santa Claus and eight carrots, each for one of the reindeer. When it's foggy, we put out an extra carrot for Rudolph. Our family hangs up stockings to be filled with goodies and Santa always leaves his footprint in the soot of the fireplace.

Phase two: you discover your own truth about Santa Claus. Somehow you figure out that Dad and Mom are putting out the gifts and the boot print in the soot is the same size as your Dad's foot. For me, it was hearing the sound of plastic candy wrappers one Christmas Eve as my Mom and Dad were hanging a string of suckers on the fireplace before I had fallen asleep. In this phase, you realize that Santa represents love and the spirit of giving.

Phase three: you ARE Santa Claus.

Jordan seemed satisfied with this answer and I assured him that Santa would surely be coming as he had every year before.

When I finished talking I realized that my answer not only revealed the truth about Santa Claus, but it was also the story of my own Spiritual Evolution.

Phase one: I heard the story when I was small. This story is different all over the world. It comes in different forms, including Hinduism, Buddhism, Bahai, Islam, Judaism and Christianity. The Native Americans learned the stories of Mother Earth and Father Sky. Ancient man worshipped the sun and there are fascinating stories of Greek and Roman gods and goddesses. Just as we fill stockings and put out cookies for Santa, each belief system has its own rituals and customs to honor its God. Each believer believes his own version is the truth.

Phase two: I discovered my own truth. This is when I developed a personal relationship with God. I began to pay attention, realizing that God is present in *all things*. My spiritual journey has been enlightening and every day I become more and more aware. I am always learning something new that makes me more in awe of the wisdom of the universe.

Phase three: We are God. (We are *Love*)

We are the human expression of God. The part of me that is *Love* is God. Every time we experience *Love* we experience who we really are. *Love* is the true nature of the soul. This is why *Love* always feels so good. In the spiritual world where we are all one in *Love*, we are one with God.

Just like the Santa story, awareness has three phases. We hear the story, we discover our own truth, we are the *I am*. Life is remembering that we are beautiful.

The following Christmas, I had a beautiful experience. One of my favorite recordings on the Christmas Series is the *Ave Maria*. It is a beautiful melody written by the French composer Gonoud using Bach's *Prelude in C* as its accompaniment.

I played the *Prelude in C* on the piano, Sam had played the *Ave Maria* melody beautifully with his flute and John created a wonderful cello part. The combination is soulful and when I listen to the recording I instantly have an incredible feeling of peace.

I had sent the song out in the form of an email Christmas greeting to all of my friends. I received an amazing response from my good friend, Carol Ann, who lives in Texas.

I had met Carol Ann 5 years before. I was distributing Nu Skin at the time and the company referred me when she called about vitamins for her son. Just a few months earlier he had been involved in an auto accident that put him in a wheel chair for life. Joshua was a potential baseball star. At 15 years old he already had scouts watching him play.

He is an amazing kid and loves music. He broke his sixth cervical vertebra and is considered quadriplegic. The doctors told Carol Ann that Josh would never have children. She insisted that he not be told despite the doctor's protest.

On the day that I sent the music greeting I received an amazing response. The Christmas greeting had my album cover, a picture of the Madonna holding Jesus and it played the *Ave Maria*. Carol Ann and I have stayed in touch over the years and I have been amazed at the things that Joshua has accomplished.

This was what Carol Ann wrote:

Dear Cindy,

I just received your Ave Maria. As I look at the picture of Mary with the Baby Jesus and listen to the beautiful music play I have tears running down my cheeks. I am thinking how perfect this is. Another two minutes and I would have missed it. I am on my way to the hospital to greet my new grand baby when it comes into the world. It's Joshua's baby. Thank you dear friend for this very appropriate gift.

Love, Carol Ann

Christmas is a time of giving, forgiving, peace and love. Friends and magical *Butterfly Moments* like this are beautiful gifts from God.

Butterfly Moments

*"Across my dreams with nets of wonder,
I chase the bright elusive butterfly of love."*
—Bob Lind

I have heard that praying is when we talk to God and miracles are when God talks to us. The story I am about to tell you is true. I believe it happened so I could pass it on to you now. I call this story *Butterfly Moments*.

Butterfly Moments are those magical moments of spiritual awareness that give us exhilarating chills. They are those times when we are reminded that we are *never alone* and the universe is always watching.

Have you ever wondered when you pray or call out to God, if anyone is listening? You hope that there is someone or something listening but you really don't know for sure. Still, because you are so incredibly desperate you call out anyway, "God Help Me!!" This was the nature of a conversation I was having with my friend, Derri, one beautiful September morning as we were walking through the woods at Moss Wright Park

As I listened to my friend, I remembered a time when I also had these doubts and questions. Derri and I were both raised in the Catholic faith. Some of the things I was taught in my religious education rang true but, then again, some things I learned were in conflict with a feeling deep inside my soul. This promoted my own spiritual search for God and I felt an overwhelming desire to share what I had learned with Derri.

I was struggling to find the words that would help her understand that we are never separate from God without sounding crazy. So, I did what I always do when I have a question… I asked.

I needed the Holy Spirit to inspire me with some kind of story that would bring light to this question. Then as *The Voice* spoke, I listened.

All of a sudden I felt a rush and my heart was filled. I became very excited and started telling Derri a kind of parable.

"OK!" I said, "Say that God is a big beautiful oak tree, and the essence of this tree instead of wood, is Love." I was completely elated and began speaking rapidly as if the message couldn't come out quickly enough. I actually had to force myself to slow down.

All of a sudden Derri quietly said, "Cindy, there is a butterfly on your shoulder." Her tone was full of awe and wonder.

"Great!!" I exclaimed. "Eastern philosophy, Native Americans and the Celts all referred to butterflies as a spiritual sign from the Creator. This means the Spirit is truly with us and it is *not* my imagination! My question has been answered and this is real! "

Derri had become very quiet and as we spoke she was constantly turning her eyes to the butterfly flipping its wings on my right shoulder. It was sitting in my blind spot, so I couldn't see it. Derri was walking on the right side of me and it was very clear that our new friend was there for *her* benefit. I went on with the story that had been inspired.

"God is an oak tree. From this magnificent oak tree is carved a flute, a bowl, a table and chairs, a dollhouse and a beautiful ornate jewelry box. Each has its own worldly value and special purpose to *serve*.

The flute plays beautiful music. The bowl serves food for the nourishment of the body. Table and chairs are used for family gatherings, desks for poets and writers and a place for signing peace treaties. The dollhouse is loved by a little girl and played with everyday. Finally, the jewelry box holds beautiful and expensive diamonds and jewels.

All of these wooden objects serve with the purpose for which they were made. However, sometimes during a gentle rain, each can remember when it was that magnificent oak tree. We are like those things that were carved from the tree. Each of us were manifested from *Love* and each of us has a different purpose."

As we walked along the pathway, we discussed *Love* and the purpose of every human being created by God. A babbling brook was singing her song near the pathway in the park and the leaves were dancing in the trees. Throughout our conversation, at different points, Derri kept saying to me every five minutes or so, "It's still there!"

Yes, amazing as it may seem, the butterfly stayed with us a good half an hour and we understood it was a loving sign from God. Looking back on that morning it seems like it was filled with magic. Everything seemed so alive in the woods that morning as I shared this memorable event with my friend. This was a Tuesday.

The following Friday morning I was walking in Moss Wright Park again, this time alone. At least I thought I was alone. I like to listen to authors like Wayne Dyer and Marianne Williamson with my Walkman and this particular day the message was about "surrendering the outcome". In other words, let go and let God.

After I had recorded all eleven CDs for the record company the company went away. It had major financial problems and had to close its doors. I was completely frustrated.

Surrender the outcome! Turn it over! I really needed to hear these words now. It's like anything. Knowing what you need to do is not of any value unless you *do it!* I began to remember another time of surrender and as I did big salty tears began rolling down my face.

"Jose Cuervo you are a friend of mine, I like to drink you with a little salt and lime." I had played the song at parties and everybody who heard it loved it! I had truly believed in my little song and I worked very hard on it. Even though the song went number one in Los Angeles, it never even hit the national music charts.

I thought of that afternoon in my living room when I was actually challenging God! "*You do it!!*" I had screamed. "I've done *everything* I possibly can! You can do mountains and oceans and solar systems. So *You* do it!!" I was frustrated that day as well and I had a definite attitude.

I remembered being on my knees and sobbing uncontrollably until a kind of peace settled over me. I had resigned my own efforts and turned it completely over to God. At the time I had no idea what I was doing. All I knew was there was nothing more I could do. Within two years Shelly West recorded *Jose Cuervo* and it became the 1983 Country Song of the year in Billboard Magazine.

Now here I was, 17 years later filled with emotion as I relived that intense moment of surrender and the promise fulfilled. I was having a great moment of enlightenment and my tears were flowing like a cleansing rain.

In the midst of this great moment I noticed a shadow hovering over my head. The sky was bright blue without a cloud in it and the sun was warm on my back. As I curiously watched the shadow fluttering around I was stunned as I watched it suddenly stop and land on my right shoulder. My shadow was tall in the sunlight. I carefully turned my body around to get a better look and clearly see its shadow as well. It was a butterfly on my shoulder!!!

I slowly turned my head around and saw a small beautiful orange and black butterfly with delicate wings on my right shoulder contently riding along with me as I continued to walk.

Now the tears were flowing like a river and I began to talk to my new friend. "I know why you're here. Thank you for being with me. You're my new best friend!"

It seemed like a moment frozen in time as I completely surrendered my new music project to the universe and the butterfly *listened*. I guess I thought as long as I kept talking the butterfly would stay. I felt exhilarated all over and there was a warm rush running through me. I know the people passing by probably thought I was acting strangely but I didn't care. In fact I hardly even saw them. I was totally absorbed with the small miracle at hand.

This story gets even better! A good 20 minutes or so had passed and the butterfly was still riding on my shoulder. I had an appointment and as I approached the van I started explaining this to my little orange and black friend. It wouldn't leave me.

I realize now that the fact it wouldn't leave me has a profound message as well. I put the index finger of my right hand up by my right shoulder and very slowly started to move it back and forth. After all the butterfly and I were such good friends that I didn't want to do anything to startle it. "I need to go, and you are not going to understand windows," I said.

THE LITTLE BUTTERFLY GOT ON MY FINGER!! I pointed that finger about 10 inches from my nose and that butterfly and I were now face to face. There was a mother and her small child on the playground nearby. I sat on a stump and continued to talk to my wonderful friend.

I knew now what Alice had experienced when she walked through the looking glass. It was as if I were in a dream. The trees never looked so beautiful and the giggle from the toddler playing nearby was like a magic song.

As it sat on my finger, the butterfly would slowly lower its delicate orange and black wings, then quickly put them back up. It did this over and over as if affirming that my request had been heard and the universe was in motion on my behalf.

Finally I said, "I really need to get going and you are not going to understand windows. This is your home and I come here to walk pretty often. I'll be back and you can visit me then".

I walked over to the van with the butterfly still on my finger and opened the door. With that, my tiny little friend lightly danced away into the sunlight.

The following Tuesday morning I was walking again through Moss Wright Park with my friend Derri. Again it was a beautiful September morning. This time I was sharing the story of the butterfly that had visited me just four days earlier.

Derri and I belong to a spiritual study group and I was telling Derri that we ought to give it a name. I said, "I like the word sacred." She said that she had read Wayne Dyer the evening before and liked the way he used the word "knowing".

I said, "How about the Circle of Sacred Knowing!"

Derri said, "There is a butterfly on your shoulder!"

There are no words to describe our awe. Derri was walking on my left side and this time the butterfly was on my left shoulder. I carefully turned my head and saw a beautiful, small orange and black butterfly sitting on my sweatshirt.

Our mouths dropped completely open as we stared at my little friend. "What do you think?" I said quietly.

She said, "I think I'm afraid *not* to call it that."

As we watched the butterfly, it put its small delicate wings down slowly, and then flicked them back up. It did this 3 or 4 times as if to say, "I promised I'd visit you when you came back and a promise is a promise."

Then, after just about a minute, it danced away into the sunlight. There were no words exchanged, only the silent knowing that is felt deep inside the chambers of your heart and soul.

Each of the three visits of the butterfly during that beautiful week in September 2000 has a different lesson. The first visit confirmed that the loving universe is always listening. Whenever we ask a question, the answer *always* comes even though sometimes it might seem it might be just your imagination.

The second visit confirmed without a doubt that we are never alone. Even when I brushed my finger on my shoulder the butterfly wouldn't leave me. We have all had desperate moments when we have cried out for help. Oh, yes, the universe is listening. When we get out of the way, and let the Divine Intelligence of God take over, miracles happen.

The third visit made this story complete. It was an affirmation that the butterfly experience was real and had a purpose. That purpose was to share this amazing story with you. When we pay attention and understand that every moment of life is precious, we heighten our awareness to the miracles of life. The little orange and black butterfly and I made a kind of pact the Friday before. The fact that the butterfly showed up again made the whole event real. No one will ever convince me that it wasn't the same butterfly that had miraculously visited me the Friday before. It was a magical moment of enlightenment and I was proud that we were friends.

Life is designed for the soul to know itself and to remember that who we *really* are is beautiful. Now I call the magical moments of awareness in our lives *Butterfly Moments*. They are those beautiful experiences that remind us that we are a manifestation of *Love*.

A *Butterfly Moment* is like the gentle rain that enables the flute, the bowl, the table and chairs, the dollhouse and the jewelry box to remember that it is really a magnificent oak tree.

Now that I have identified these moments, I realize that I have had many in my lifetime. We have *Butterfly Moments* every day and when you know this, each new day is a celebration of being alive!

Oh, by the way, this is not quite the end of my butterfly story. Two months after that memorable moment of complete surrender in Moss Wright Park I signed a new record contract.

While working on product development the company sent me the covers to the New Beginnings Series. This was the piano music project for pregnant women to play for their infants *in utero*. The three album covers, *Our Miracle, Our Playtime* and *Our Sleepytime* all had lovely pictures of new mothers and babies on the covers. I was pleased to see that there was a small orange and black butterfly in the bottom right corner of each of the 3 CDs.

When the president of the company called to ask me how I liked the covers, I told him I was thrilled. "I especially love the way you put the butterfly on the covers in honor of my butterfly story."

After a quiet pause he replied, "What butterfly story?"

Elusive Butterfly
—Bob Lind

You might wake up some mornin'
To the sound of something moving past your window in the wind
And if you're quick enough to rise
You'll catch a fleeting glimpse of someone's fading shadow
Out on the new horizon
You may see the floating motion of a distant pair of wings
And if the sleep has left your ears
You might hear footsteps running through an open meadow

Don't be concerned, it will not harm you
It's only me pursuing somethin' I'm not sure of
Across my dreams with nets of wonder
I chase the bright elusive butterfly of love

You might have heard my footsteps
Echo softly in the distance through the canyons of your mind
I might have even called your name
As I ran searching after something to believe in
You might have seen me runnin'
Through the long-abandoned ruins of the dreams you left behind
If you remember something there
That glided past you followed close by heavy breathin'

Don't be concerned, it will not harm you
It's only me pursuing somethin' I'm not sure of
Across my dreams with nets of wonder
I chase the bright elusive butterfly of love

Across my dreams with nets of wonder
I chase the bright elusive butterfly of love

Butterfly Moments of Inspiration

United We Stand, Divided We Fall

*"Infinite wisdom has seldom sent any man
into the world better fitted for his mission
than Abraham Lincoln."*
—Frederick Douglas
1865

The date is July 3, 1863. The American Civil War has been raging for two long years. It has never been completely defined why each side hates the other. Some say the war is about slavery; others say it is about state's rights. All the Confederates know is that the only good Yankee is a dead Yankee and the Union hates "Johnny Reb" just as much.

President Abraham Lincoln waits in solemn anticipation for word on the battle being fought in Gettysburg, Pennsylvania. For three bloody days Americans have been slaughtering and murdering each other. From the beginning of this gruesome war, Lincoln has seen it as brothers killing brothers and he is very sad.

In a Confederate assault known as Pickett's Charge, a man from Mississippi, screams a blood curdling "Rebel yell" as he aggressively charges, ready to kill any Yankee who gets in his way. He is tired and hungry, but somehow the hate and rage has distorted his judgment and he is ready to kill and mangle any Union soldier that he can. He has forgotten the value of human life.

The soldier from Mississippi comes face to face with a soldier in a blue uniform. The Union soldier is from New York City, where his wife and two small children await his return. In a blinding rage, the man in gray rams his bayonet into the New Yorker's chest.

The man in the blue uniform falls and the soldier in gray rams him again and again until he is satisfied that the Yankee is dead. He screams that bloodthirsty Rebel yell once more. With pure darkness in his heart he looks at the dead Union soldier and bellows, "Say hello to the devil and burn in hell, you Yankee son of a bitch!" He smiles an evil smile at this egotistic illusion of victory and moves forward to kill again.

Inside the Confederate soldier from Mississippi was a loving *silent observer* quietly watching.

On July 4, 1863, after three bloody days, the South reported 3,903 dead, 18,735 injured and 5,425 missing, for a total of 28,063 casualties. The North reported 3,155 dead, 14,259 injured and 5,365 missing for a total of 23,049 casualties. The grand total of casualties at the Battle of Gettysburg was 51,112 Americans. We were truly a nation divided.

The date is September 11, 2001. There is a man in Mississippi drinking his coffee and reading his morning paper. His sister calls and frantically tells him to turn on the news. She is crying as she reports, "They have bombed the World Trade Center and the Pentagon!"

He runs to the television set and quickly turns it on. He sees that one of the world trade towers is on fire, filling the New York sky with black smoke. In horror he watches as a 767 Boeing jet crashes into the second tower and, later, as the building implodes and falls.

Is this happening? Are those people jumping out of windows? Oh my God! He watches in disbelief as the twin towers one by one crumble to the ground. People are screaming. The fear and chaos burns a dark hole that penetrates deep into his soul.

He is stunned at the surreal picture of destruction. A golden retriever senses his master's grief and the faithful friend puts his head on the man's lap and quietly whimpers. The man in Mississippi pats him on the head.

Trained in trauma and rescue, the man instinctively starts to assess the situation at hand. He starts thinking of people who might be trapped under the rubble. The man in Mississippi has trained his dog to retrieve survivors in emergencies. He looks at the retriever and declares, "We're going to New York!!" With that he quickly packs a bag and clears out his savings account. Within an hour, he is driving on the road headed towards New York City to do everything he can do to help.

Inside the rescue worker from Mississippi is a loving *silent observer* quietly watching.

The world looked on with horror at the results of the terrorist attacks. It was a violation that affected people everywhere. It ignited human emotions everywhere and stores sold out of flags as Americans proudly displayed their patriotism. We were a nation united.

What is the difference in the Confederate soldier from Mississippi who killed the Yankee at Gettysburg and the rescue worker from Mississippi who cleaned out his account and was willing to risk his life to save lives in New York? One reacted with the darkness of ego and one reacted in the light of *Love*.

In 1863, the North fought against the South. Each side was convinced that God was on its side. In 2001, Islamic terrorists murdered innocent people because of religious belief. The United States and its allies retaliated. Each side is convinced that God is on its side.

If there had been television in 1863, and the man in Mississippi had seen the twin towers in New York crumble to the ground, would he have cheered?? The thought is almost unimaginable. In fact, the terrorist act brought a stronger sense of unity to Americans, as well as our allies from other nations. Oneness is the nature of the soul. When we experience this, the soul sings in celebration and everything seems right. Unfortunately, it sometimes takes a catastrophe for this to occur.

Love and hate are both invisible and both extremely powerful! Love is the presence of God and hate is the false illusions of the ego.

Humans hate other humans because of race, religion, economics and geography. Socrates said, "I am a citizen of the world!" Wouldn't it be lovely if everyone on the planet lived life with that in mind?

When we focus on our differences, the ego will do whatever it takes to be right. According to science, it is proven that at the physical level we are 99% percent the same. At the spiritual level, we are exactly the same. Just as the sun doesn't choose on whom it shines, God doesn't choose who is loved.

The ego judges and condemns. It is the source of jealousy, hate, conceit, greed and low self-esteem. The ego keeps the chaos alive and puts darkness in our souls. It confuses us with trickery and gives us a totally false sense of priorities. The ego gives the false illusion that we are "better than" or "not good enough".

Life is beautiful when you finally realize that your ego is your biggest enemy. This is the ingenious part of God's plan that enables us to discover what we *aren't*. The more you can identify the presence of ego, the easier it is to recognize the absence of love.

Here's how you can test whether a situation has the presence of love or ego. If it doesn't feel warm and fuzzy, and you have a hundred reasons to justify your action or reaction, it is ego. Ego is the absence of God. It is based on fear and feeds off presumed differences. Ego judges and reacts with hate.

If the action or reaction feels warm and fuzzy and there is no judging involved then it is *Love*. Love is the presence of God and the true essence of the soul. Love sees all things as having equal value and sees differences as being the "spice of life". *Love* does not judge, *Love* only loves.

"What race are you?" I love to fill out questionnaires that ask this question. It usually gives a choice of White, Black, Hispanic, Asian, Native American or other. I always write in the word HUMAN where it says "other". Other? What is up with that??

When people ask me where I worship I say everywhere I am. If they ask what religion I am I say, "I don't have one. This would limit me to learning how other people celebrate God."

My daughter, Julie Lynn, lives in Grenoble, France. She loves Europe and sees it as a big playground. She is constantly confronted with "you Americans… " I am very proud of her and her attitude of learning from other cultures. Exploring our differences makes for a better understanding of our similarities. I have discovered that as human beings, we are all essentially more alike than different. However, when we focus only on our differences we create a breeding ground for conflict.

No one ever wins in war, which comes in all different forms. It doesn't matter whether it is domestic, street gangs, business related or national. It is human violation that is in complete opposition of who we really are. Someone always gets hurt and because we are one in spirit, if one of us is hurt, it affects the whole.

Revenge never feels good to the spirit. It might be temporarily satisfying but a violation is still a violation. When we hurt someone, it puts a dark hole in our soul that can only be healed with love. Years later the guilt will get you. When you have been violated or have violated, it might show up later in the form of a cancer or some other dis-ease. Forgiveness is the only cure.

Love can be used as a powerful weapon. If you want to win anything, start with *Love*. You will have the strongest power of the universe on your side. It is a force so powerful that it can actually disarm the atomic bomb! When in any kind of confrontation the solution is always, "What would love do now?"

The date is April 9, 1865. The Confederate soldiers have launched an attack on the Federal troops in Farmville, Virginia. General Lee looks at his men. They out numbered 3 to 1. Many are barefoot and thin from hunger. All further resistance is futile, and Lee orders the white flag of surrender (made from a white towel) be carried through the Union lines.

Lee dresses in his finest uniform, and with the last bit of pride in the south, he meets with General Grant at the Appomattox Courthouse to negotiate the terms of surrender. After four long, bloody years and one and a half *million* casualties the Civil War is finally over.

It is a blessed day and all are relieved of the duty of hating each other. General Grant offers to share food rations to feed the hungry Confederate soldiers. Just that morning, they were ready to murder each other. The United States is united again and the soldiers are eating together in peace. They are experiencing the beauty of surrender.

Surrender is the ego's enemy. It gives the illusion of admitting defeat and weakness. I would suggest that he who surrenders to invoke peace is the greater of the two. This is what the Masters know. Jesus said, "Love your enemies." From peace, love has the potential to blossom and flourish. Nothing can grow in the darkness.

"United we stand, divided we fall." This is true of everything that is. We are one with the universe and it is from this that we get our power.

When we bask in the light of *Love*, it is a beautiful *Butterfly Moment*.

INVISIBLE

"Farewell' said the fox.
'This is my secret, it is very simple:
You can only see with your heart.
The essence of things is invisible to the eyes."
—A. De Saint-Exupery
(The Little Prince)

I am a member of Toastmasters International. It is a great organization that promotes taking the fear out of public speaking. We give speeches, evaluate speeches and earn awards. Each speech that we give, teaches us a lesson in using different tools when we speak. Some of these include voice inflection, eye contact and animated body language.

It was my turn to give a speech and my assignment was to use props. A few days before the Toastmaster meeting, I was driving around thinking about what I would speak on. All of a sudden, I got this great idea! It occurred to me that the most important things in life are invisible, and I was going to bottle them up for all to see.

I went to the Dollar Store and bought six big transparent containers. They cost a dollar apiece. When I walked into the Toastmaster meeting, one of the gentleman members came up to me and asked very innocently, "So, Cindy, how much did you pay for those big jugs?" Lee didn't mean anything by it. This is a very nice man who teaches music at a private school and plays the organ at his church.

The answer I *could* and probably *should* have given was, "They cost me a dollar at the Dollar Store."

I just couldn't do it.

Nope!

I couldn't resist.

Before I knew it, that mischievous part of me I call CJ, took over, and ceased the opportunity.

"Ex-cuuuuuuse me??" I replied.

It was great! We all laughed, including Lee. He is known for always telling corny jokes. This turned out to be the funniest thing any of us ever heard him say!

I put the most powerful forces in the universe in the "jugs." All of them are *invisible*. On the lid of each of the clear, gallon sized containers, I wrote a word to label its content. The words were, WORDS, THOUGHT, MUSIC, ENERGY, LIFE and LOVE.

When I began my speech, I had everyone stand, and put their hands behind their back so they could not see any part of their bodies. This is what I said:

"Imagine that you are an alien from another planet and you just popped into this human form to study life on earth. You have never seen a mirror so you don't know what you look like. Now look around the room. You see all kinds of other human forms and they are all very different. Which one are you most like? Are you female or male? What color is your skin? What color is your hair? Do you have hair? Are you fat or thin? How many eyes do you have? How old are you?

I went on. "THIS is who you are. THIS is the real you. You are not your form. What you *really* are is ageless and weighs nothing. It is made of life and spirit. It is the "being" part of you, the soul that is one with God.

Disassociating yourself with your "form" can be a very powerful exercise. It helps to get in touch with the *silent observer* that inhabits your body. I have personally used this exercise in many ways. When you become aware of your invisible self, you realize that you can become one with anything.

I have become one with rain, snow and wind. I have floated on my back in the breakwater and become one with the ocean. When I want to become one with the earth, I lay on a warm sandy beach or a grassy field of green with my eyes looking up to the sky. Being aware of my oneness with everything makes me feel like there are no limitations to what *I am* or what I can be.

Have you ever realized that the most powerful elements in the universe are invisible?

One day, in Redondo Beach, my brother Mark taught me something that has stayed with me throughout the years. We were sitting in the front seat of his car that was parked in front of the house we grew up in. I remember, it was a red BMW and he was very proud of it. I was in my late twenties and Mark was in college. I was complaining that someone had said some horrible things to me that deeply hurt me. Word for word I repeated the vile language that this person had used.

Mark looked at me and grinned. "Cindy, put two fingers in front of your mouth and repeat what you just said". Looking at my two fingers in front of my mouth, I repeated the hurtful words again. I remember it made me feel sick with pain.

"Look at your fingers," Mark said still grinning. "What happened to them??"

"Nothing," I said.

"Are you sure? They didn't burn or fall off?"

"No," I said as I felt a shift in my perception. Mark was giving me what I refer to now as a *Butterfly Moment of Inspiration*. Mark had made me realize that *I* was the one who had given power to the words. The words themselves had no power. *I* was the one who had given permission for the vile words to penetrate and hurt.

Words are invisible. When someone says words that can hurt us, they don't have power unless we *choose* for them to have power. If someone says something you don't like, DON'T TAKE IT PERSONALLY!! After all, the words came out of *their* mouth. It's *never* about you. It's *always* about *them* and what is going on in *their* life.

If someone dumps garbage in your yard, do you keep it?

No!!

It stinks!!

When we allow ugly words to penetrate our being, we accept someone else's garbage as our own. Sometimes we even wallow in it and let it pollute our day by getting hurt, angry and resentful.

Usually, I find that people, who are rude or antagonistic, have some kind of conflict going on in their lives. When we react with *compassion* instead of anger, it is incredibly empowering. I have learned to quietly send a blessing to my attacker's troubled spirit. It takes some practice, but, the more you do it, the easier it becomes.

Words can also be empowering. Sometimes, all it takes is for someone to say, "You can do it!" These four little words can make all the difference in accomplishing things we never thought possible.

Thoughts are invisible. They are the magical seeds of dreams that come true. A thought is the origin to every creation and discovery known to man. Thoughts are the source of every action and attitude that we have.

Thoughts are incredibly powerful and *will* manifest themselves. With this in mind, it is important to be careful of what you think. Henry Ford once said: "If you think you can or if you think you can't, you're right. "

Music is invisible. It is the universal language. Musicians and composers use music to translate the deepest of human emotions. Music communicates in a way that can be understood by everyone. It has the power to heal and wake emotions in the human spirit.

Life is a beautiful symphony to be enjoyed. The earth has a continuous orchestration of sound that makes music all around us. The songs of the animals, the rushing of a river and the wind whistling through the canyons are all part of the universal song expressing the miracle of life.

Music can make us feel like dancing. An opera can bring emotional tears to our eyes even when it is sung in a foreign language. A mother's gentle lullaby can put a baby to sleep as it communicates a message of love.

Energy is invisible. Over 98% of our physical being is made up of empty space consisting of invisible energy fields holding the molecules of our body together. Energy is the universe in motion. It is energy that makes the heart beat, the sun shine and the earth rotate on its axis.

Life is invisible. It is what leaves the body when the body dies. Life is the force that makes the trees green, the flowers bloom and our eyes shine. Life is a precious gift from God. God *created* life in order to *experience* life. Without life, there is no-thing.

Love is invisible. It is so powerful it can disarm the atomic bomb!

Love is the true essence of the soul. Love can cure any dis-ease and solve any conflict. I use love as my Excalibur, a magic sword that wins every battle. There is nothing greater than *Love* because there is nothing greater than God and God *is* Love.

Remember that the most powerful forces of the universe are invisible. You have access to them all. Use them with care and you will manifest amazing miracles!

Healing With Music

"We long to make music that will melt the stars"
—Gustave Flaubert
1821–1880
(Madam Bovary)

It was around 4:00 in the afternoon that unforgettable day when I heard the fax line ring four times. No fax came through but I remember thinking that I should have answered it. About ten minutes later, the fax line rang again. This time I answered the phone. I heard a man's voice on the other end ask if this was the correct number for ordering Cynthia Music. I got very excited as artists do when someone is interested in their creations.

I told him that I was the composer, Cynthia. "I'd like to order eight *Celtic Journey* CD's," said the man. Then he made a strange kind of sound like he was clearing his throat.

"Sure! May I get the address that you would like them shipped to?" He started to tell me and made the sound again. This time I realized that he was crying. It was a deep sobbing cry like I had never heard.

"I'm sorry," he said, and then the man cried a little more. "I am buying the CDs for the pallbearers at my son's funeral. We played the *Celtic Journey* music throughout the visitation. The music was so beautiful and I want them all to have a copy."

I could feel warm tears falling down my cheeks. My heart was full of love and emotion and I could feel his deep sorrow as our spirits came together.

The man's name was Bill Fain. His son, Robbie, had been killed in a fire at the young age of 22 years. It was obvious that there was much love and Robbie's death was a tremendous loss to him. I told him it was a great honor to be part of such a sacred event for people I had never before met.

I had forgotten that the fax number was temporarily being used on the *Cynthiamusic* website. It was amazing that I even picked up the phone!

These are the moments of my personal triumph. Awards, number ones, or how much money you have in the bank are not valid measures of success. These are the illusions of the ego. Success is about making a difference and touching people's lives.

A few weeks after the phone call, I received a copy of the letter that was sent to the pallbearers along with the *Celtic Journey* CD. I'd like to share it with you now. These are my awards of success and they are absolutely precious to me.

A letter by Bill Fain

Janet and I received many positive comments about the calming and beautiful music we played during Robbie's visitation. We would like you to accept as a gift, from Robbie and from us, this CD, Celtic Journey. It was the only music we played that evening during the visitation, which was scheduled from 6:30 to 8:00, but actually lasted until 10:00, when the last of the family and friends finally reached us.

As you may know, Rob was becoming more and more intrigued with his Irish heritage, and spoke of traveling to Ireland. Robbie enjoyed this music. We hope you will also, and when you listen to it, we trust it will help you with the healing we all must go through. But we think this music will enable you to remember Robbie as you knew him in your own unique way, as well.

An interesting footnote occurred that gives evidence to that "sense of connectedness" Steve mentioned during the funeral message. When Janet and I decided we would like to make a gift of the CD to a few special people, I got on the Internet to see how I could acquire several copies. I eventually found a website and a phone number for Emerald Eagle Music. (www.cynthiamusic.com)

I called and the fax machine answered, so I thought that was that. I assumed I would have to find another way to get copies of the music. About ten minutes later, against my normal nature, I called again. This time a voice answered, and I felt an immediate "connectedness" with this unknown person. When I told her that I wanted to order several copies of Celtic Journey she was very pleased. She asked why I wanted so many copies, and I told her in my stumbling fashion. She was touched beyond my expectation, so I asked, "Who is this?" She said, "This is the composer, Cynthia." She just happened to be there and decided to answer the phone

With some emotion, after a little conversation, I struggled to say goodbye and God Bless. And I was struck by the unusual feeling, that even at this time, Robbie is continuing to touch others, allowing us to feel a "connectedness" with people we have never met... and yet feel that we've known for a long time.

Bill and Janet Fain

I have received many wonderful letters from all over the world from people who have used my music for different reasons. Dentists, doctors and massage therapists have written to me telling stories of patient recovery and stress relief that the music seems to promote. I have teachers who have reported using the music in classrooms during tests. I had one letter from a kindergarten teacher who used the music to settle the children down when they were wound up and restless.

In my research, I learned why the *Cynthia* music has such a calming effect on the human spirit.

First, the music is transparent. This is important because any kind of lyric or word suggestion can trigger a negative emotion associated with a bad memory.

Secondly, the music is played on a piano. This provides a large range of different tones. The high notes stimulate the mind. The low tones bring peace and relaxation and they can actually make you drowsy. Our solar plexus responds to the middle notes.

Finally, the music is played in a flowing motion and an easy kind of rhythm that can physically bring down the heart rate and normalize the rhythm of breathing.

All I know is that I followed God's lead and found the music in what I refer to as the pure source of *Love*. It is with a loving spirit that I play the piano and I like to think of myself as a fountain spilling love on all who hear my music.

All of us need each other to experience love. Thank you for being part of my experience. As you hear my compositions, listen for the love.

The music is there to remind you that *we are all Love*. It is from this mystical place that we can see heaven on earth where butterflies dance to the *uni-versal* song of life.

The Rosebush

*"You will find more in the woods than in books.
Trees and stones will teach you
that which can never learn from masters."*
—Saint Bernard
1091–1153
(Madam Bovary)

Every year, my mother's family has a reunion in Pahrump, Nevada, a town about 50 miles outside of Las Vegas. We have family who live there and those of us who don't stay at the Saddlewest Motel and have a big time! One thing about Mexicans, they certainly know how to party!! In fact, it's been so much fun, my dad's side of the family has joined the group.

We always have our reunion on Father's Day weekend. On Sunday morning, several of the family members go to the Catholic Church to attend Mass. I remember a conversation I had with my young cousin, Chris, one year as we saw them leave for church. The conversation has always stuck with me.

We were sitting on a patio when Chris asked, "Cindy do you think it's important to go to church?" His family had never really gone and he was unfamiliar with the experience.

"It depends what you are looking to accomplish by going to church," I answered. "If you are asking if you have to go to church to know God, then the answer to your question is NO."

We were sitting in front of a beautiful rose bush. "All of the answers about life and God can be found right in front of you at any moment of your life. Take this rosebush, for instance." We both focused on the lovely pink flowers growing on the bush.

As I began to speak, I felt I was being inspired by the Holy Spirit. I was having a *Butterfly Moment of Inspiration* and I could feel my heart fill and a surge of peace and divine knowledge rush through my spirit. I was awake and my soul was rejoicing in celebration.

I was talking and *listening* at the same time. "Where did the rosebush come from? This is a miracle in itself. How did the little rose seeds know to grow into this beautiful bush? Look at the roses. See the mature flowers whose petals are falling as they slowly lose their fragrance and beauty to return to the earth to fertilize the plant."

I began pointing at the rosebush. "From there, the dead flowers will be reborn into those tiny little baby rosebuds that are still inside the green. Some of them are beginning to open and we can see just a hint of pink color peeking through. The young rose buds are pink and closed up tight. It is not yet their time to be beautiful. They are the children. And, then, there are those gorgeous pink roses that have already bloomed, inviting you to smell their wonderful fragrance.

Even from where we are sitting, we can smell the aroma of the beautiful pink flower as she turns her head to the sun. She knows it is her time for magnificence and glory! We know we can't grab her and pluck her from the bush or we will be pierced by her thorns. This is part of her perfection and the evidence that her divine creator has given her the ability to protect herself. The rosebush provides pleasure to the human senses. When we harvest the rose we give her as a symbol of love and, when we do, she rejoices. This is because her purpose is fulfilled. See, Chris, you don't need to go to a building to find God because God is everywhere! Today, church is in this rosebush."

We sat there for a timeless moment staring at the beautiful flowers with completely different eyes. They are the spiritual eyes, the windows of the soul that enable the *silent observer* to experience the human mind, heart, and soul.

The *silent observer* witnessed an enlightening moment for me. Chris is twenty years younger than I. The *silent observer* saw the teacher and the student in both of us. Because of Chris's question, we were both enjoying the lesson. Both of us were sharing an appreciation for the mystical beauty of life. The lesson was simple and beautiful.

So many times I hear people say they get nothing out of church, and so they don't attend. Some even call themselves atheists. The God that has been presented to them is judgmental and vengeful. This is in conflict with the nature of the soul. The soul identifies God as unconditional love. Therefore, people get lost because they can't accept what they are told as truth.

Sometimes it takes something dark to happen in our lives before we look for God. Maybe it's a crippling accident, a serious illness or an unexpected death of someone we love. The first thing we do is call out for "GOD!!" The soul knows that God is the light in the darkness. God *allows* the darkness when the spirit is lost. The darker the dark, the easier it is to find God's light.

A wise man once said, "People go to church because they are afraid *not* to." Where did this thinking come from? Is it because they feel guilty if they *don't* go? Wouldn't this make God's love conditional?

Which one of your children would you throw into an inferno?? For eternity no less! Why would you believe God would throw His children into fire? I don't see God as vengeful. The God I know is only *Love*.

I hear people say things like, "I *hope* my prayers will be answered." What prayers are *not* answered? Sometimes the answer might not be our choice, but we have to trust that it is the best choice.

There is a big difference between *believing* in God and *knowing* God. I once heard a great analogy of the difference between knowing and believing. Mr. Johnson *believes* that these eight children that he is taking to MacDonald's are all his. As they are sitting there enjoying their Happy Meals, Mrs. Johnson *knows* that they are hers.

The saddest thing I hear is people telling me that they don't completely trust God. They have some kind of doubt that God loves them unconditionally and wants them to be happy and enjoy life.

When someone tells me this, I ask this question. "Is there someone in your life, who was supposed to love you, who somehow betrayed you?" The answer is always, "Yes" and, sometimes, it is said with tears.

One evening, I met a woman who was really struggling with trusting and understanding God. I learned that not only had her father abused her, but also he had abandoned the family.

I asked the woman, "Do you think of God as *God the Father*?" "Yes," she answered.

"Do you have children?"

She told me that she had a little girl who was seven years old.

"Do you love her?"

"Of course, I do," she said with a glow of warmth and motherhood in her beautiful dark eyes.

Then, I said very slowly and gently, "Maybe because you know what the love of a mother is, you can think of God as *Mother God*. Then you can envision a beautiful woman lovingly holding her baby in her arms."

"I never thought of God like that," she said.

I felt a peace come over both of us as she quietly nodded her head and said, "I can do that. Thank you." It was a *Butterfly Moment* shared by two souls who have experienced the beauty of motherhood.

Church is a wonderful place to celebrate in fellowship in the light of God's love. I have met some of my best friends in church. However, it is important to find a church that teaches God's *unconditional* love. This is the only love that is real.

There once was a ten-year-old sage who was considered to be enlightened. One day, his elders challenged him with a trick question. The elders asked the young sage, "Where is God?"

The boy looked at them with clear, sparkling eyes and said, "Tell me instead where God isn't!"

The next time you see a rosebush, a tree or even a stone, look for God. You just might have a *Butterfly Moment!*

SACRED SEX

*"Male and female have the power
to fuse into one solid,
because both are nourished in both,
and because the soul is the same thing in all living creatures,
although the body of each is different."*
—Hippocrates
460–377 BC
(Regimen)

Today is February 9, 2002. My parents just called me from Pismo Beach. As the endless waves were making their way to the shore, Daddy put his cell phone up so I could hear the music of the ocean. "Can you hear it Cindy? It's the most beautiful sound on the earth!!"

I asked if he was honeymooning with Mom. "You betcha! I am here at this beautiful place with the most gorgeous woman in the whole world!" These are my parents after forty-nine years of marriage. I am a lucky girl!

When I was eight years old, my mother told me the most beautiful definition of a sexual orgasm I have ever heard. Of course at the time, I had no idea what she was talking about! Mom had gotten a book with little fuzzy ducks and we were having that memorable mother-daughter talk about the birds and the bees.

As she described the process I remember first thinking how in the world can you manage to do that?? Second, I felt grateful that my parents were willing to do something that seemed so weird and personal to make us. Third, because my parents had four children I assumed that they had sex a total of four times in their lives. After all, who in the world would ever want to do something like that unless they absolutely had to??

As mother explained the biological facts of the reproductive process, I listened in fascination. Even at this young age, I remember being in awe of the mystical miracle of life. However, this was all new to me and my eight-year-old mind was trying to take it all in.

Mother asked me if I had any questions. I looked at her with complete innocence and asked, "Can you feel when the sperm goes to the egg? How do you know when this happens?"

I'll never forget the look on my mother's face. It was a quiet smile full of womanhood and beautiful wisdom. She looked at me with a sparkle in her eyes and said, "Oh, yes, Cindy. You know. It is like walking into a great big meadow full of beautiful flowers that all open up at once!"

Of course, this statement only confused me more, but I never forgot it. Later on, when I fell in love, I learned that my mother was right. I feel very fortunate to have been blessed with a mother who understands sex is beautiful and sacred.

I like to refer to the sexual act as the "procreative dance." I believe that sex is one of God's most beautiful gifts. Sex is playful, fun, pleasurable and very spiritual. Because of its many pleasures it keeps the human species alive.

When we perform the sexual dance, erotic human passions ignite. This makes sex a wonderful way to celebrate being alive! Biologically, sex actually produces chemicals that create powerful energy that helps maintain good health and youthfulness.

Sacred sex has all of the ingredients for spiritual awareness. While making love, the body, heart and mind can experience timelessness, oneness, deeply-felt emotion, freedom, sweet surrender, unlimited creativity, expression of love and the feeling of connectedness. Enjoying sex as a sacred experience is heaven on earth.

So, when is sex sacred? Sex is sacred when the woman sees and appreciates the man as divine and the man sees and appreciates the woman as a goddess. Sex is sacred when we feel free to use our bodies as a vessel to take us to the enchanting world of spirit. Sex connects the spirit and the body into one. Sacred sex is seeing the "God energy" which is the "Love energy" shine from the eyes of your partner. It is a magnificent expression of love with spirit that can take us to better understanding the vastness of the sacred universe.

A beautiful body is nice but it certainly is not the most important thing for enjoying great sex. Everyone's body has special places that trigger erotic pleasures. Sacred sex is about finding and knowing these secret places on your lover as well as yourself. The goal is to please your partner and make it a good experience for him or her. It is in the giving that we receive. Communication is key. You should ask what your lover likes and share what pleases you. For sex to be good, *it absolutely has* to be a two-way street. Sex can take you to a wonderful world full of new discoveries! Experiment and have fun!

I can only speak from my experience as a woman. The best lovers I have had are the ones who take their time to please. There is nothing like the feeling of being worshipped and adored. Attitude is most important. The goddess takes a little more time to arouse but for those of you who have mastered this, you know that when she is aroused, the effect has certainly been worth it!

When I play the piano, in a way I can say that I am, making love. This is because music can take me to the same beautiful place of awareness I go to when I have a passionate sexual experience with my lover. Like music, the sacred sexual dance is the expression of the love I feel deep in my soul. Both are sacred, beautiful ways for me to communicate these deep feelings of love.

Making love is like making music. For instance there is a definite rhythm pattern in sex. The primordial sound expressed during sexual intercourse is our song at the most primitive human level. Like music, sex is an expression of emotion and passion, which is also the expression of our spirituality. Just as music is an art, creative sex is an erotic art that can be used as a way to heal the spirit and the body.

Making love can make us more aware of our spirituality. When we are lost in sacred sexual expression we lose track of time and any sense of separateness. We completely lose our individuality and become as one with our partner. In this mystical awareness, we can better comprehend our oneness with the universe.

I am very happy that I am a woman and I love to express my feminine energy with the sacred sexual dance. I remember an enlightening moment I had while standing on the Tor at the Isle of Avalon. I was with my golden friend Lerin and we were looking out over the small valley where the town of Glastonbury, England lies. She told me something beautiful that brought a new awareness and sense of sisterhood with the feminine energy of Mother Earth.

"Look at her womanhood." Lerin said. The Tor (which is a hill) and Chalice Hill (the hill next to the Tor) can be viewed as two breasts". She pointed across the small valley to Wayward Hill where stands a lonely thorn tree. Legend says that the tree was planted by St. Joseph of Arimathea by placing a staff on the ground, which was made from the tree that provided the thorns for the crown made for Jesus at his crucifixion. "The long hill over there is like her leg folded under. The remains of the Abbey in Glastonbury can be seen as being in her womb."

It was an enlightening moment. As we looked across the beautiful, green English landscape, I could see the form of a woman's body lying on her back with her face to the sun. I could feel the soft yet powerful spirit of what the locals refer to as the Goddess. The Goddess is the feminine loving energy of God. She loves us like a mother and her spirit beats in the heart of Mother Earth.

All humans are made up of both male and female energies. The Goddess is our feminine spirit just as God the Father is our male spirit. Women celebrate their sexuality in the spirit of the Goddess. She receives the seed in an act of sweet surrender that fills her soul with joy and sense of purpose. The female's soft energy is the heart opened in the expression of love.

Men celebrate their sexuality in the spirit of The Father. He plants the seeds to create and multiply which fulfills his sense of purpose. The male's strong energy is thought. It is the creative spirit in the expression of love.

Sex gives men and women the opportunity to experience the other's energy. This exchange of energy is electro magnetic. When we make love, we are no longer man and woman. When sex is sacred, two become as one and it gives the human spirit the satisfaction of feeling complete.

Sex helps us to comprehend our oneness with the universe. In sexual union, we are God and Goddess energies expressed as one in Love. In the sacred act of making love when we celebrate our partner as divine, we dance the most sacred of dances to the music of the universe! These beautiful dances are some of my most treasured Butterfly Moments.

> *Grassy fields along the stream*
> *Call to make our bed,*
> *I have made a place for us*
> *Come and rest your head.*
> *Listen to the river sing*
> *Its ancient lullaby,*
> *A poetry two lovers bring*
> *When by its shore they lie.*
> —Cynthia

You Make Beautiful Love With Your Eyes
—Cynthia Jordan

The sun is slowly rising
There's a fire in the sky
We didn't go to bed all night
And the wine bottle's dry
I've never felt like this before
It feels like paradise
You make beautiful love with your eyes

(chorus)
You make beautiful love with your eyes
And I feel my heart coming alive
We barely even touched but I've never felt love so much
You make beautiful love with your eyes

We must have been lovers,
Somewhere long ago
When you look at me this way
I can feel you touch my soul
This is familiar from another place in time
You make beautiful love with your eyes

You make beautiful love with your eyes
And I feel my heart coming alive
We barely even touched but I've never felt love so much
You make beautiful love with your eyes

❦

In God We Trust

"Who then to frail mortality shall trust"
—Francis Bacon
1561–1626
(The World)

Summers in Redondo Beach are awesome! As I was growing up, I hardly missed a day going to the beach with family and friends. We would go down at 11 o'clock every morning and come home about 3 in the afternoon to eat. When Dad would get home from work at 4:30, we would be off again to go swimming and body surfing with him. We practically lived at the beach.

When we were teens, my brother Steve and I liked to hang out at the breakwater in Hermosa Beach. We had a lot of friends who surfed and the surf was always good there.

Steve and I had a black bicycle. It wasn't fancy and it didn't even have gears but I loved that bike. When I was a kid, stingray bicycles were the "thing". They had butterfly handles that were high at the handles and dipped down low in the center. Steve put a butterfly handle bar on that black bike.

Every morning Steve would ride me to the beach on the handlebars of that black bike. I would sit on the beach towels and off we'd go. I remember the first day we went down Francisca hill. I got a scary, *I don't know about this*, kind of feeling. Steve just said, "Hold on!" and I did.

As we sailed down the hill, I remember that feeling of exhilaration. My hair was blowing in the wind and butterflies were fluttering all around inside my stomach. By the time we crossed over Pacific Coast Highway I knew that Steve was not going to let anything happen to me. Every day after that I couldn't wait to get on those handle bars. Steve was in full control and I felt safe and secure. I completely trusted my brother and I was able to enjoy the ride!

Where there is complete trust there is no fear. Have you ever thought of the way we trust complete strangers? For instance, we trust that the drivers from oncoming traffic will not cross the double yellow line. When we go out to eat, we trust that the people in the kitchen haven't contaminated the food.

We go on amusement park, elevator and airplane rides without the second thought that they might be fatal. Yet so many people I speak to don't *completely* trust God. They use the word "hope." You never hear them say, "I hope no one crosses over the double yellow line" or "I hope this food is not poisoned" or "Gee, I hope this elevator doesn't crash"? Sometimes I think we trust strangers more than God.

Freedom is the nature of the soul. When there is complete trust we are free of fear. When we completely trust God and the wisdom of the universe, it is the most wonderfully liberating feeling there is. After all, what is it that God *can't* do?

I have heard the words *gullible* and *naïve* used for people who "would believe anything." To me, they have the innocence of a child. I have learned that people who don't trust others probably can't be trusted. Lack of trust is usually a result of some kind of betrayal by someone who was supposed to love you. Maybe it was a parent, a lover, a friend, or a relative. People will lie because they've been lied to. This causes fear to set in. When we focus on fear, life can turn into a living hell.

Many people have a fear of flying, especially after the terrorist attack on September 11th. This is because they feel out of control. But when are we really ever in complete control of anything?

Every day, people are killed in car accidents, but, does this mean you won't get in a car? You might say, "It's OK as long as I'm driving." What about the other guy? A few months ago I was in a bad car accident. Someone made a left hand turn directly in front of me and we had a head-on collision. When it happened, I thought I had seen the light, but within a few moments, I realized that it was the air bag. I had on my seat belt, and, between that and the air bag, I was able to walk away from the accident.

I remember that as soon as my accident occurred, the first thought I had was, "There's a blessing here. I don't know what it is now but I trust You completely and I know this happened because You love me. There is something that needs to be realized from this and I'll know what it is in time."

I have learned to trust God. It is a *complete feeling* of trust, just as I had with my brother Steve as he rode me on those handlebars down Francisca hill. Complete trust is the most liberating feeling you can have! When you *know* that everything happens in your life so that you will remember that you are *Love,* then nothing "bad" can happen.

Several weeks after my accident, I realized there were many blessings and lessons learned. A month later, almost to the day, a good friend of mine was also in a car accident. In an attempt to miss a deer, my young friend Dylan ran into a tree. Right before impact Dylan called to God, "I want to live!" Dylan is only 22 years old and is now a quadriplegic. The blessings from this accident are much more difficult to understand. Dylan knows that he has a special mission in life and his attitude is amazing. He is one of my greatest teachers and it is an honor to know him.

When we are challenged with tragedy, the flame of love is ignited. The community support for Dylan and his family has been beautiful to watch. Look at all of the *Love* that poured out to the victims and their families after the terrorist attack in New York on September 11, 2001. People drove thousands of miles to help. The Red Cross could hardly handle all of the blood donors. People from all around the world sent money. When tragedy happens to one of us, it happens to all of us.

Just for a moment, imagine this scenario. A spirit is about to be given an opportunity to have the human experience. It has heard that this is a beautiful experience because humans are fascinating beings who can comprehend *love.*

Now let's say that God is like a travel agent and, together with the spirit, they plan a beautiful journey to discover that they are a manifestation of *Love.* They have a meeting where it is decided on what gender and physical features the human form will have, where it will be born and who the parents will be.

God then asks the spirit how it would like to experience love. The spirit gives a long list that includes things like mother's love, romantic love, love for a child, unconditional love, friendship, and the list goes on. Together they plan challenges so the soul can learn things like forgiveness, compassion, and trust.

Because God is Love, the spirit recognizes love as a burning flame. Every time the spirit experiences love the flame ignites. The greater the love is, the bigger the flame. When the spirit experiences fear the flame disappears to a glowing ember.

At some point, the human realizes it has this spirit. This is a grand epiphany when the human understands that the spirit is part of the soul of God. In this moment of enlightenment, the human finally catches on that *everything* that happens is the soul's experience of life and Love.

Bad things don't happen. Your life is in perfect harmony with the intelligence of the universe and there is a blessing in everything. Your journey is designed for you to discover who you are. Challenges are our best teachers.

Freedom is the nature of the soul. Complete trust in the wisdom of God is the definition of complete freedom. We are made from Love. Just as the flute carved from the tree is still the tree, we are a manifestation of Love.

Every moment of life is a *Butterfly Moment* because in every moment of life, God is experiencing Love through you. It is in the Love experience that we sing the universal song as *one*.

A Final Note

"This little light of mine,
I'm gonna let it shine!"
—Hank Williams Sr.

You are a precious miracle. Your body is a sacred vessel that is home to the divine spirit within. From the moment that you entered this world, you have had a purpose. Just as a small pebble makes a continuous ripple in the sea, your life will make a difference in the tapestry of time.

The world is like a house of mirrors. The mirrors hold the answers to enable you to remember who you *really* are. It is your *divine self*. You are a golden light of *Love* that can shine bright as the sun. So is everyone else. Look for that shimmering light in everyone. I promise it is there! When the shadow of fear darkens their spirit, silently shine your love light on them even brighter. Their soul will recognize it and you will be what I refer to as "*Doing the God Thing*". Fear is the enemy. Love will always empower you.

Butterfly Moments can occur in any second of your life. Anytime you wish to experience one, simply become quiet and listen to the silent voice of God. It is your true voice, the silence between the musical notes, the silence between every heartbeat and the silence between every precious breath of life. As my daughter Denise said after returning from the *other side*, "The light of God is everywhere, Mommy. People just can't see it."

Don't look for God outside of yourself. Instead, listen to the loving voice that speaks to you from within your heart. Trust God and look for the miracles. They are everywhere! Remember the beautiful lesson of the little orange and black butterfly…

You are *never alone!*

Many Blessings to you and those you love!
Your friend,
Cynthia

Please send your Butterfly Moment stories to:
Butterfly Moments
PO Box 1501
Hendersonville TN 37077
Or email us at cynthiamusic@msn.com